ARTIFICIAL INTELLIGENCE IN DENTISTRY

DR. PRIYADHARSHINI D

DR. JAGAT REDDY .R.C.

DR. VANDANA S

DR. JOHN BALIAH

Clever Fox
PUBLISHING

Chennai • Bangalore

CLEVER FOX PUBLISHING
Chennai, India

Published by CLEVER FOX PUBLISHING 2021

ISBN: 978-93-90850-97-6

This Book is Dedicated to My Mother Abirami and Father Dhandapany

Contents

Foreword

It is a privilege for me to contribute the Foreword to *Artificial Intelligence in Dentistry* by Dr. Priyadharshini D. I am happy to see that the author has written and organized the complete topic of Artificial Intelligence in Dentistry into a single book. This is an incredibly helpful book since it makes the topic simple, lucid and understandable. The author was able to present the contents in a comprehensive manner. The book is created and written in a clear, comprehensive and concise manner.

This book's distinguishing feature is that the author has catered exclusively to AI research in dentistry, making it a very useful resource material for the entire Dental fraternity. I am confident that this book has been written to fulfill the needs of all aspiring clinicians and academicians by including all the relevant theoretical and practical application of AI in dentistry. I congratulate her on the successful publication of this book.

Prof. Dr. Saravana kumar
Principal
Department of Periodontics
Indira Gandhi Institute of Dental Sciences
Sri Balaji Vidyapeeth University
Pillaiyarkuppam
Puducherry

Preface

The goal of this book is to identify how Artificial Intelligence (AI) can be used in Dentistry. This book is particularly of use to early learners helping them understand and relate AI to dentistry. The use of artificial intelligence in dentistry is still in its early stages. AI is growing at a steady 40% growth pace annually in the healthcare industry, which is anticipated to reach $6.6 billion by 2021. [1] Extensive research pertaining to AI and its usefulness reduces burden of healthcare professionals. As a consequence of the assessments, AI research applications in dentistry and healthcare should be approved for everyday practice on scientific grounds.

DR. PRIYADHARSHINI D

Date

Acknowledgments

I thank God, Almighty for giving me the strength and courage to complete the given task. Sincere and true salute to my grandmother Visalatchi T, my father Dhandapany N, my mother Abirami T, my uncle Sandirasegaran N, my aunt Amirtham T, my brother Premragunathan D, my sister Manasa, my brother Madhavan, family and friends.

I am truly and deeply indebted to my guide Dr. R.C. Jagat Reddy, M.D.S., Professor and Head of the Department, and my Co-Guide Dr. Vandana. S, M.D.S., Professor, Department of Oral Medicine and Radiology, Indira Gandhi Institute of Dental Sciences, Pondicherry, for their guidance and discussions in this venture.

I sincerely thank Dr. John Baliah, M.D.S., Reader, Department of Oral Medicine and Radiology, Indira Gandhi Institute of Dental Sciences, Pondicherry, for guidance, motivation, and discussions which had always been a source of encouragement during every step of this venture.

I am thankful to Dr. Sivasankari T, M.D.S. Reader, Dr. Rajkumar M.D.S. Senior lecturer and Dr. Anusha M.D.S., Senior lecturer Department of Oral Medicine and Radiology, Indira Gandhi Institute of Dental Sciences, Pondicherry for their valuable support and encouragement.

I sincerely thank Er. Prabakaran J, B. Tech, MBA., for his guidance in technical aspects of Artificial Intelligence.

I thank my colleagues for their help and motivation.

Introduction

Artificial Intelligence[AI] are a group of technologies that helps machines and computers to simulate human intelligence. A broad range of disciplines in recent years including health care have been found to use AI. [2] John McCarthy was the first to coin the term AI in a conference on the subject held at Dartmouth in 1956. An important field in computer science is AI which creates complex machines with the characteristics of human intelligence.

Two types of AI are General (AI) and Narrow (AI). General AI is machines that can think, reason, see and hear like humans. In movies like Star Wars (think C-3PO, a droid programmed for etiquette and protocol) cannot be achieved by this time but Narrow AI can be achieved in which technologies will perform specific tasks better than humans. These AI are derived from deep learning and machine learning that has improved performance in various areas that include facial recognition, text analysis, image classification, speech recognition with increased applications in areas such as natural language processing, autonomous vehicles, and collection of a set of technologies in medicine.

Due to advances in learning algorithms, computing power and large availability of datasets sourced from wearable health monitors and medical records AI plays an increasingly vital role in medicine and healthcare. There is an increasing rate of AI in the health care market of about 40% and is expected to reach \$6.6 billion by 2021. The efficiency and effectiveness of patient care can be improved by the development of the new application by AI with help of health care data. [1] There is numerous type of AI in health care such as machine learning – deep learning & neural networks, natural language processing, physical robots, rule-based expert systems, robotic process automation. [3] It is a powerful tool to be used in healthcare as it can aid in the prediction and diagnosis of disease, collection, and storage of patient data leading to accurate and reliable results. In health care, the application of AI focuses on various branches such as electronic health record analysis, image analysis in radiology, pathology, dermatology, ophthalmology, cardiology, neurology, obstetrics. [4] The pioneer in this field is IBM Watson that has made promising progress in oncology. [5] AI is a useful modality in classifying and screening suspicious altered oral mucosa which would undergo premalignant and malignant changes and diagnosis and treatment of lesions of the oral cavity. The superiority of AI is to detect even minute changes at a single-pixel level that might go unnoticed by the naked eye and no observation fatigue is seen. AI that involves the omics data analysis and individual medical profiles may predict a genetic predisposition for oral cancer for large populations accurately. AI algorithms can be used in long-term treatment outcomes, personalized medicine, recurrences, and survival of oral cancer patients can also be calculated using AI. Zhang et al hypothesized that the intraoperative pathological diagnosis would be the margin accuracy and real-time in resection surgery in which the results would be even better or comparable.[6]

According to Palma et al, oral microbial volatile organic compound signatures would be detected by AI that has important applications in periodontal medicine practice and oral microbiology. Biomechanical preparation of the root canals with precision can be obtained if it is integrated with Endodontics. Precise detection of occult metastasis and comparative analysis of immunohistochemistry and other techniques and analysis of digital slides by AI can be achieved with eliminated subjective and observer bias that is perceived in the diagnosis of epithelial dysplasia. AI might improve Digital imaging methods integrated with radio diagnosis and reduce observer fatigue. [7]

The teaching and learning process can intensely make up the way students recognize knowledge with the incorporation of AI. Designing of meaningfully differentiated curriculum to error-free evaluation pattern can be contributed by the AI. The cost of education and burden on educators can be reduced with AI-based education [8]. AI aids as assistance and conserving time for patient care to dentists. The traditional doctor-patient relationship will not be replaced by the AI-based system instead it will augment patient care. [2] Online assistants (such as Siri), search engines (such as Google search), and games (such as AlphaGo), into numerous fields including medicine. [9]

In oral health, it aids as a decision support system in various branches such as

1. Prediction and diagnosis of disease
2. AI-assisted extraction
3. Cephalometric analysis in orthodontics
4. The precision design and chairside manufacture of dental prosthesis based on the tooth cusp assessment
5. Investigate dental material
6. Robotic surgery
7. Bioprinting
8. Computer-Aided Design – Computer-Aided Manufacturing [CAD – CAM] in the precision of dental prosthesis
9. Early detection of oral cancer
10. Facial pain analysis
11. Dental image analysis
12. Automatic detection of the panoramic image
13. AI-assisted labeling of the tooth in [Cone Beam Computed Tomography [CBCT] and prediction of periodontally compromised teeth.

Evolution of Artificial Intelligence

"Success in creating AI would be the biggest event in human history. Unfortunately, it might also be the last, unless we learn how to avoid the risks."
—*Stephen Hawking, Theoretical Physicist*

The history of formulation, research, and development of AI has numerous tributaries. [4] In 384 -322 BCE Aristotle was the first to present the concept of AI in history. A direct view of the emergence of machinery which could replace humans was not given by Aristotle, but his logic centred on syllogism that could identify the thinking method of the man. [10] In 1308, Ramon Ilul a 14th century Catalan poet and great missionary theologian published a book based on the idea of Aristotle named Ars generalis ultima (The Ultimate General Art). It was about recreating the minds of man utilizing mechanics based on Aristotle's logic [11]. In 1738 displayed his mechanical duck that could quack, flap its wings, paddle, drink water, and eat and "digest" grain. In 1844, Robert-Houdin found that Vaucanson's duck discharge was prepared in advance in the which was a sort of gruel composed of green-colored bread crumbs. Vaucanson's duck is a remarkable piece of engineering apart from the excretion. [11]

George Boole in 1854 said that logical reasoning was performed in the same way as a solution of the equation with a set of systems, that will assure confidence in the possibility of complete replacement of logical thinking and computing. [4] In 1950, Alan Turing introduced the Turing machine project which was the beginning of AI. He introduced the concept of the imitation game, or Turing Test. [13]

In 1955 the term AI was used in the studies on contemporary AI in the United States. This term was introduced in workshops by John McCarthy at Dartmouth University, Nathaniel Rochester at IBM, Marvin Minsky at Harvard University, Nathaniel Rochester at IBM, Claude Shannon at the Bell Telephony Institute. [14] In 1943, a paper was published by Warren McCulloch and Walter Pitts named neural networks as a way to imitate human brains. [15] In 1951, the stochastic neural analog reinforcement calculator was developed by Minsky and Dean Edmunds which was the first neural network in history [16]. For the first time in history, the AI program was developed in 1955 by Allen Newell and Herbert Simon [17]. The Logic theorists program, a work co-authored by Whitehead and Russel proved 38 of the first 52 axioms of Principia Mathematica. [12]

Arthur Samuel first introduced the term Machine Learning in 1959. Arthur Samuel defined machine learning as the "field of study that gives computers the ability to learn without being explicitly programmed". [18] Hubert Dreyfus in 1965 carried out the research to find out the fundamental problems in strong AI which he emphasized in his book. He commented every person has the area in the mind which works in a way that cannot be achieved by the computers. [19] AI program called ELIZA was developed by Joseph Weizenbaum between 1964 -1966. [20] ELIZA helped people to communicate in English with the machine. Based on the program these machines aid in communication with people on a superficial level without the deep understanding of self-consciousness. It is used in the imitation game as the minds of those participating in the game were emotionally assimilated with the machine in the dialog. [21] Arthur Bryson and Yu-Chi-Ho accelerated the research and development which focused on implementing weak AI. [22]

In 1969 back propagation algorithm was developed. The backpropagation algorithm made a decisive contribution to the implementation of today's deep learning. The AI self-execution algorithm was improved with help of the back propagation algorithm that utilizes a partial derivative approach that is implemented in a propositional and symbolic way. [23] The AI moved from the Turing test implementation, logical and mathematical verification to real-life use based on the concept of Machine Learning [4]. An early expert system emerged in 1972 that enables non-specialists to use knowledge by organizing and processing expert knowledge in a specific field. [24]

In 1972, the expert system named MYCIN was developed at Stanford University it aids in the identification of bacteria that are the causes of serious infections and presents antibiotics that are suitable for them. Initially, the expert system implementation was focused on the medical field and it reflected the high utilization of AI in the medical field [4]. In 1976, Computer scientist Raj Reddy introduced his work on Natural language processing and this was the first continuous speech recognition approach. [25] In 1978 John. P. Mc. Dermott of Carnegie Mellon University was the first to introduce XCON [eXpert CONfigurer] which was the production rule-based system. It aided in the ordering of DEC 'S VAX computer systems automatically, it selects the components of the computer system based on the customer's requirements. [26]

In 1980, WABOT 1 [27], Greenman [28], Saika [29], ASIMO [30], Nexi [31], P1, P2[32] [33] are humanoid social robots with head, neck, and cameras constructed in place of eyes. In 1982, a fifth-generation project was developed in Japan. A fifth-generation project was developed for knowledge information processing. [34] In 1986, at the University of Massachusetts, a decision support system called DX plain was developed. DX plain will aid as the decision support system that would list probable differentials based on the symptom complex. It also aids the medical students as an educational tool. [35] In 1993, GERMWATCHER an expert system was developed that could detect nosocomial infections. GERMWATCHER applies the Centers for Disease Control's National Nosocomial Infection Surveillance culture-based criteria for detecting nosocomial infections. [36] In 1995, A.L.I.C.E (Artificial Linguistic Internet Computer Entity) was developed by Richard Wallace. A.L.I.C.E was inspired by Joseph Weizenbaum's ELIZA program but it has the addition of natural language sample collection on an unprecedented scale, enabled by the advent of the web. [37] Later ALICE was an inspiration for various chatbots includes Apple's Siri, Google Now, Microsoft's Cortana, Facebook Messenger, Amazon's Alexa, Telegram, and many more. Even though Joseph Weizenbaum invented chatbots to deliver health care, now chatbots are being used to support and scale business teams in their relations with customers in various industries. [38]

2

Artificial Intelligence in General perspective

"Some people call this artificial intelligence, but the reality is this technology will enhance us. So instead of artificial intelligence, I think we'll augment our intelligence."

—*Ginni Rometty, CEO of IBM*

DEFINITION

Artificial intelligence (AI) is the term used to describe the use of computers and technology to simulate intelligent behaviour and critical thinking comparable to a human being. [39]

Bellman R et al 1978 defined [AI] as the study of algorithms that give machines the ability to reason and perform cognitive functions such as problem-solving, object and word recognition, and decision-making. [40]

Panch T et al in 2018 defined [AI] as, a broad scientific discipline with its roots in philosophy, mathematics, and computer science that aims to understand and develop systems that display properties of intelligence. [41]

[AI], in general, is defined as the capability of a machine to imitate intelligent human behaviour. [42]

Russel et al defined it as a branch of computer science that attempts to both understand and build intelligent entities, often instantiated as software programs. [43]

Artificial intelligence (AI) is defined as intelligence exhibited by an artificial entity to solve complex problems and such a system is generally assumed to be a computer or machine. [44]

TYPES OF ARTIFICIAL INTELLIGENCE

There are two main types of AI: 1. STRONG AI & 2. WEAK AI

1. STRONG AI

Albus et al 1991 defined it as "the capacity of a system that can act appropriately in an uncertain environment". [45] It is also called artificial general intelligence that can function in the same way as human intelligence and it can replace the intellect of the person with necessary principles. The principle here refers to the structure of human intelligence that can be purely digitized by computing. [46] Computer has the potential to completely replace the human mind if every thought of the person is implemented in a conditional and propositional way that can be unambiguously synthesized formally and logically rather than in principle. The computing machine autonomously and actively will have the ability to recognize and understand the object sub-consciously. [4] Copeland M et 2016 commented that General AI, which has machines that can think and reason and even see and hear like humans. This concept which can be seen in movies like Star Wars (think C-3PO, a droid programmed for etiquette and protocol) is not something we can achieve at this time. [2]

2. WEAK AI or NARROW AI

Weak AI means a system in which human beings take advantage of some medical and logical mechanisms in which intelligence works to efficiently execute intellectual activities that a human can perform. [46] Copeland M et 2016, Narrow AI in which technologies exist to perform specific tasks as well as, or better than, humans. This intelligence was derived from the AI techniques such as Machine Learning and deep learning. These AI technologies helps in facial recognition, image classification in radiology, speech recognition, text analysis, autonomous vehicles, etc. [2]

BRANCHES OF ARTIFICIAL INTELLIGENCE

There are several different branches of AI namely,

1. Machine learning – neural networks and deep learning
2. Natural language processing
3. Fuzzy logic
4. Rule-based expert systems
5. Physical robots
6. Robotic process automation

1. MACHINE LEARNING - NEURAL NETWORK AND DEEP LEARNING

Machine learning is a technique that uses the training models and learns from the models to interpret the outcome. They depend upon the large data sets of training models with the known outcome for feeding. Deep learning and neural networks are complex forms of machine learning. Deep learning predicts the outcome of many variables and features. [3]

Example: Machine learning techniques are used to predict the apical lesion of the teeth. [47]

2. NATURAL LANGUAGE PROCESSING

The text analysis, speech recognition, translation, and goals linked to language use machine learning technology for natural language processing. A large frame of the language data should be learned by machine learning for the NLP. The interpretations, understanding, creation, published research, and clinical documentation classification involve NLP. They evaluate unstructured clinical notes on patients, transcribe patient interactions, prepare reports and conduct conversational AI. [3]

Example: IBM Watson has integrated NLP for speech recognition, text analysis, and translation. [48]

3. FUZZY LOGIC

Fuzzy logic is alike to human intelligence which analyzes and gives significance to terms like "often", "higher" and "smaller". The absolute values and the uncertainties are present in the real world, to overcome this the fuzzy logic system is used as everything cannot have a linear function. These fuzzy logic systems assisted with the computer-aided system are used for applications in the field of medicine. [49] These systems are used in diagnosing dental diseases by training the data set of the diseases for the system to arrive at diagnosis through a sequence of questions.

Example: In dentistry, the color-changing after the post bleaching was detected by the fuzzy logic system. [50]

4. RULE-BASED EXPERT SYSTEM

Expert systems are commercially used and were one of the dominant technology in the 1980s. It is based on the IF-THEN rule. They are widely used in health care as clinical decision support systems over decades. A set of rules and their systems are provided by the electronic health record (EHR). A knowledge domain is created by human experts and knowledge engineers build a series. This expert system with a large number of data can conflict and can cause interruption. It is time-consuming and difficult if the knowledge domain is changed. Based on the machine learning algorithm and the data availability they are replaced in the health care system. [3]

Example: Visual Basic expert system was developed to help the postgraduate students in the diagnosis and treatment of the most common and rare oral ulcers. [51]

5. PHYSICAL ROBOTS

Physical robots are well-acknowledged and each year more than 200,000 robots are installed around the world. Predefined tasks like dispensing supplies in hospitals assembling objects in places like factories, lifting, welding repositioning. These robots are trained to aid in the tasks. AI skills are being set in their operating system. The physical robots perform with the same intelligence as other areas of AI. The robotic surgical procedures include head and neck surgery, prostate surgery, and gynaecologic surgery. [3]

Example: Computer-Assisted Surgical Planning and Robotics (CASPAR), Robotic Arm Interactive Orthopedic System (MAKO Surgical Corp RIO), ROBODOC used in orthopedic surgery. [52]

6. ROBOTIC PROCESS AUTOMATION

Robotic process automation performs using an information system. They are easy to perform transparent in their actions and inexpensive compared to other forms of AI. The computer programs on the servers are used and robots are not used in this automation. They depend on business rules, a presentation layer, and a combination of workflow integration systems. The repetitive tasks in healthcare like updating patient records, prior authorization, and billing are performed using robotic process automation. They are merged with image recognition and other technologies and can be used to extract data. They are being combined and integrated with other technologies as image recognition is being integrated with RPA and robots have AI-based 'brains'. [3]

Example: Surgical robots in Computer-Aided Surgery [CAS] and image guidance aids surgeons to acquire adequate lesion information to achieve precision diagnosis and surgery planning. [53]

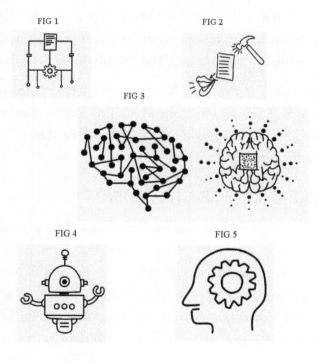

FIG 1: Fuzzy logic, FIG 2: Natural language processing, FIG 3 : Machine learning , FIG 3 : Robotic process automation, FIG 5 : Expert system

	3

HOW AI WORKS?

"I imagine a world in which AI is going to make us work more productively, live longer, and have cleaner energy."

—Fei-Fei Li, Professor of Computer Science at Stanford University

AI works on the self-learning mechanism through learning methods such as

- MACHINE LEARNING
- DEEP LEARNING

• MACHINE LEARNING

Machine learning is a statistical technique for fitting models to data and to 'learn' by training models with data [3]. The ability of a computer to learn from experience, i.e. to modify its processing based on newly acquired information. The neural networks are the more complex. This process can be based on a simple decision-making tree such as if-then, which leads to a conclusion, or using deep learning algorithms which imitate the human brain in processing several types of data and creating patterns for use in decision making through neural networks [54].

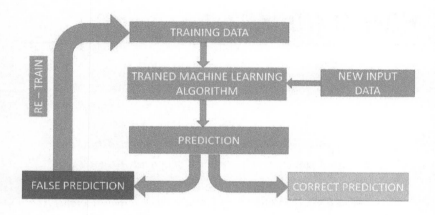

MACHINE LEARNING ALGORITHM FLOWCHART

• DEEP LEARNING

Deep learning is a form of machine learning with numerous features. Deep learning is a process in which an algorithm receives data (i.e. excel charts, images, etc.) and then examines the data according to a predetermined pathway such as Artificial Neural Network [ANN] that was developed specifically to solve the desired task. Deep learning is a subset of machine learning which is structured similar to human brain processing, taking into account multiple data sets at the same time, which are evaluated and reprocessed for second and third different evaluations and so on, until reaching an output. ANN - the input is entered into a set of algorithms and their output is re-entered to a different set of algorithms to reach the final output. The ANN is developed according to a training set of data provided to train the algorithm to answer a specific question. The training data set must represent the problem it is being asked to solve, to ensure an accurate result. Convolutional neural network (CNN) - a specific type of ANN, typically based on deep learning algorithms with several hidden layers to analyze data. Multiple hidden layers exist in CNN so the relationships between layers are complex so the term convolutional [10].

MACHINE LEARNING AND DEEP LEARNING

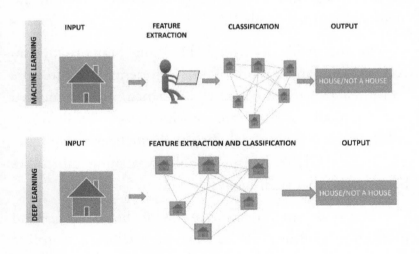

In 2010, IBM Watson, a computer running software designed by IBM Research, was introduced by Ferrucci D et al. Watson is a computer system that could compete in real-time on the American TV quiz show Jeopardy at the level of a human champion. Watson excelled at human expert levels in terms of precision, confidence, and speed on the Jeopardy quiz show after three years of intensive study and development by a core team of around 20 researchers. Their findings clearly showed that DeepQA is an effective and flexible architecture that can be used to combine, implement, evaluate, and advance a wide range of algorithmic approaches to rapidly advance the field of question answering (QA). [55]

Min H et al in 2010 commented that "AI has shown great promise in improving human decision-making processes and the subsequent productivity in various business endeavors due to its ability to recognize business patterns, learn business phenomena, seek information, and analyze data intelligently." [56]

In the field of Group Decision Support System (GDSS), an application of service-oriented architecture and intelligent technologies was designed. They combined artificial intelligence technology with users and GDSS in a collaborative setting, concluding that intelligent techniques can handle GDSS transportation dispatching difficulties better than other traditional solutions. [57]

In a systematic literature review of the challenges and promising solutions for barriers to Intelligent Tutoring System [ITS] in both formal and informal settings, such as student basic computing skills, hardware sharing, mobile-dominant computing, data costs, electrical reliability, internet infrastructure, language, and culture, it indicated that there is immense potential for future opportunities. [58]

Kaplan et al in 2018 defined [AI] as a system's ability to correctly interpret external data, to learn from such data, and to use those learnings to achieve specific goals and tasks through flexible adaptation. They presented the potential and risk of AI using a series of case studies involving universities, corporations, and governments, using the lens of evolutionary stages (artificial narrow intelligence, artificial general intelligence, and artificial superintelligence) or focusing on different types of AI systems (analytical AI, human-inspired AI, and humanized AI). The Three C Model of Confidence, Change, and Control, they concluded, is a framework that helps businesses think about the internal and external consequences of AI. [59]

4

AI in Healthcare

"What all of us have to do is to make sure we are using AI in a way that is for the benefit of humanity, not to the detriment of humanity."

—Tim Cook, CEO of Apple

Application of Artificial intelligence in medicine has led to immense progress in the field of the health care in terms of research and patient care.AI has improved precision in routine procedures. It is very useful in collecting all the health care data. This will be time-consuming in hospitals where more patients are attended.

A literature report suggests VISualizatIon of Time-Oriented RecordS (VISITORS) system was studied which includes tools for intelligent retrieval, visualization, exploration, and analysis of raw time-oriented data and derived (abstracted) concepts for multiple patient records, 1000 oncology patient records were studied by a group of 10 users- 5 clinicians and 5 medical informaticians. There were no significant differences between the response times and between accuracy levels of the exploration of the data using different timelines. They concluded that intelligent VISITORS system is usable, feasible, and functional. [(60)]

Guidi G et al designed an artificial Intelligence-based Computer-Aided Diagnosis system for the analysis of Heart Failure patients to assist the clinical decision of the non-specialist staff. This system had the patient's pathological condition and highlights possible aggravators of heart failure. The system is based on three functional parts: Diagnosis (severity assessing), Prognosis, and Follow-up management. The database from the period 2001–2008 with a total of 136 records from 90 patients, including baseline and follow-up data were included in the study as inputs for training data. This system helps in monitoring scenarios by automatically providing outputs readable even by non - cardiologist physicians and nurses about the severity and type of Heart Failure. [(61)]

Another study by Bennett CC et al was based on the dynamic decision networks and Markov decision processes that learn from clinical data and develop complex plans via simulation of alternative sequential decision paths with artificial intelligence framework for simulation of the environment for exploring various healthcare policies, payment methodologies, and form the basis for clinical artificial intelligence. Their results were significant as the AI model was cost-effective compared to conventional treatment plan. They concluded that an AI simulation framework can approximate optimal decisions even in complex and uncertain environments when the proper design and appropriate problem formulation is done. [62]

In a literature report by Gulshan V et al, developed an algorithm for automated detection of diabetic retinopathy and diabetic macular edema using a deep convolutional neural network. 128175 retinal fundus photographs were used for training and validation with separate data by 7 certified ophthalmologists of the US board. They concluded that deep machine learning had high specificity and high sensitivity for detecting referable diabetic retinopathy. [63]

Diabetes was predicted by El-Jerjawi et al using ANN in a study where several factors were prudently studied and coordinated with an appropriate number for coding. These factors were categorized as input variables and output variables that reflect some possible levels of disease status in terms of the assessment system. The data were entered into the Java Neural Network tool environment, which determined the value of each of the variables using Java Neural Network, then the data were trained, validated, and tested. The diabetes dataset contains 1004 samples with 9 attributes. This model was first used to determine the value of each of the variables using Java Neural Network. After training, validating, and testing the dataset, we got (87.3%) accuracy, the average error was (0.010), the number of epochs was (158,000), several training examples were (767), and several validating examples was (237). [64]

Haenssle et al detected melanoma with help of CNN which was carried out in Google's Inception v4 CNN architecture, it was trained and validated using dermoscopic images and corresponding diagnoses and compared with 58 dermatologists. The comparative cross-sectional reader with a 100-image test-set was used Level-I: dermoscopy only; level-II: dermoscopy plus clinical information and images. But their results revealed dermatologists outperformed the CNN. Since the training data sets for CNN are limited it was not able to detect melanoma. [65]

AI Clinical decision support system of Watson For Oncology [AI CDSS WFO] was compared concordance with multidisciplinary tumor board for breast cancer by Somashekhar SP et al. They used the treatment recommendations provided for 638 breast cancers between 2014 and 2016 at the Manipal Comprehensive Cancer Center, Bengaluru, India. WFO provided treatment recommendations for identical cases in 2016. A blinded second review was carried out by the center's tumor board in 2016 for all cases in which there was no agreement, to account for treatments and guidelines not available before 2016. Treatment recommendations were considered concordant if the tumor board recommendations were designated 'recommended' or 'for consideration' by WFO. Their results revealed that there was 93% of breast cancer case concordances. They concluded that the AI clinical decision-support system WFO may be a helpful tool for breast cancer treatment decision-making, especially at centers where expert breast cancer resources are limited. [66]

In diffuse gliomas, a machine learning method was implemented to predict the isocitrate dehydrogenase (IDH) genotype by Wu S et al. In this study, 8 classical machine learning methods were evaluated in terms of their stability and performance for pre-operative IDH genotype prediction with a total of 126 patients for analysis. 704 radiomic features extracted from the pre-operative MRI images were analyzed. Patients were randomly assigned to either the training set or the validation set at a ratio of 2:1. Machine learning had the superior prediction of the IDH. [67]

5

APPLICATIONS OF ARTIFICIAL INTELLIGENCE IN DENTISTRY

AI has made a revolution in the field of medicine and dentistry. The use of technologies in the field of dentistry has been steadily progressing. It can be applied in various fields of dentistry based on the needs of the specialty. AI assists dentists with patient care, treatment planning, and in some cases, they are also used to perform dental procedures.

I. ARTIFICIAL INTELLIGENCE IN ORAL MEDICINE AND RADIOLOGY

According to ADA, Oral and maxillofacial radiology is the specialty of dentistry and discipline of radiology concerned with the production and interpretation of images and data produced by all modalities of radiant energy that are used for the diagnosis and management of diseases, disorders, and conditions of the oral and maxillofacial region. AI in oral medicine and radiology can be used in various perspectives such as diagnosis, radiological assessment, and treatment planning. Many studies which have been conducted in the field of oral medicine and radiology had high sensitivity and specificity. The high success rate of AI was seen in the field of radiology which aids in radiological diagnosis.

Literature evidence suggests recurrent aphthous ulcers were predicted using a genetic algorithm optimized neural network. It comprised of 96 patients, Group 1 including 86 patients for the construction phase and Group 2 comprising 10 patients for the reproduction phase. Their literature findings exhibited a 90% accuracy rate in recognizing recurrent aphthous ulcers. They concluded that the Genetic Algorithm might be used to predict recurring aphthous ulcers. [68]

Maghsoudi et al conducted a study using an intelligent system based on the ANN to predict the most common and dangerous oral diseases such as oral leukoplakia, oral lichen planus, and oral squamous cell carcinoma. A total of 150 patients were chosen from 50 people for each illness. The four traits that were shown to be common in diseases were chosen and encoded to the range [0,1] before being given into the algorithm. Artificial neural networks were found to be a strong approach for diagnosing and predicting oral and dental illnesses as a consequence of the study's findings. [69]

In a study, vascular disorder Hereditary Hemorrhagic Telangiectasia (HHT) was diagnosed using the ANN and Infra-red spectroscopy. Fourier-transform Mid-IR spectroscopy was used to acquire IR spectra from blood plasma from HHT patients and a healthy control group. Artificial neural network (ANN) studies and visual inspection of scatter plots of the dominating main components were used to process, classify, and evaluate spectral data. Their findings indicated that HHT has a disease-specific IR-spectrum that is considerably different from the control group, and that Mid-IR-spectroscopy combined with ANN analysis may diagnose HHT with a sensitivity and specificity of at least 95% with a conclusion that IR-spectroscopy in conjunction with ANN analysis can be considered as an alternative diagnostic approach. [70]

In the education of dental Postgraduate students regarding the diagnosis and treatment of most common and rare oral ulcers Virtual Basic expert system was implemented by Ali SA et al. Burkett's Oral Medicine (2008), Morris' Strategies in Dental Diagnosis and Treatment Planning (2004), and a variety of healthcare websites such as Mayo Clinic were used to compile the knowledge database. The expert system was created using Visual Basic Ver. 5 languages, and the generated program was copied to CD-ROMs and sent to 60 Tanta University Faculty of Dentistry postgraduate dental students and house officers, along with a questionnaire about the assessment. Their findings indicated that they had a success rate of 75%, the expert system worked well in terms of diagnosis and treatment strategies. [51]

Probabilistic Neural Network and General Regression Neural Network (PNN/GRNN) was designed for early detection and prevention of oral malignancy by Sharma et al. The oral cancer database, which included 35 characteristics and 1025 entries, was used to create their model. To identify malignant and non-malignant patients, all clinical signs and history are taken into account. The data for 1025 patients were obtained using a nonrandomized or nonprobabilistic technique, as was all of the data in the registries throughout five years. The information is gathered from Tertiary Care Centre Cancer Registries, OPD (Out-Patient Department) datasheets that record clinical details, personal histories, and habits of patients, as well as the archives of Departments of Histopathology, Surgery, and Radiology. Their findings indicated that the total accuracy for training data was 80% and for validation data was 73.76 percent, with 34 predictors deemed to predict survival, thus the PNN/GRNN data mining technique can be created for early diagnosis and prevention of oral cancer is appropriate. [71]

Gene Expression Profiling and Machine Learning predicted oral cancer in a study. In 86 of 162 OPL patients who were recruited in a clinical chemoprevention experiment with the incidence of oral cancer development as a predetermined goal, the gene expression profile was evaluated. Oral cancer-free survival was linked to gene expression patterns, which were utilized to create multivariate predictive models for the disease. [66] Support vector machine (SVM), Regularized Least Squares (RLS), multi-layer perceptron (MLP) with backpropagation, and deep neural network were the four classification algorithms utilized in this study (DNN). Fisher discriminates analysis was used to pick relevant features from the gene expression array. With one sample cross-validation, they found that DNN had high accuracy (96 percent) whereas SVM and MLP had 94 percent accuracy. [72]

Song et al designed a low-cost, portable, easy-to-use smartphone-based intraoral dual-modality imaging platform was developed to classify the image based on auto fluorescence and white light images using deep learning methods. The auto fluorescence and white light picture pair's information is retrieved, computed, and merged to feed the deep learning neural networks. These picture pairs were collected from 190 individuals that visited the emergency room. Oral oncology professionals classify these pictures as normal, oral premalignant lesions (OPML), or malignant lesions as suspicious. The Convolutional neural network is then used to classify the pictures. For the deep learning image classification approach, there are 66 and 64 training sets for normal and suspicious images, respectively, and 20 validation sets, because of the blurred pictures, poor focus, and excessive salinity, the remaining images are not utilized. They found that combining fused data outperforms using either white light or auto fluorescence images alone and that employing a smartphone-based approach is less costly. [73]

In a literature report by Shamim MZ et al , Oral precancerous tongue lesions were automatically detected using deep learning for early diagnosis of oral cavity cancer. Clinically annotated photographic pictures were used to generate the custom dataset. Using an image search engine, images of the various oral tongue lesions were gathered from the Internet. Before the model training procedure, they were scaled to the DCNN [Deep Convolutional Neural Network] models' necessary input picture size. Prediction models based on AlexNet, GoogLeNet, Vgg19, Inceptionv3,

ResNet50, and SqueezeNet architectures were created using 160 training pictures (80%) and their performance was assessed on 40 validation images for categorizing tongue lesions as benign or pre-cancerous (N=2) (20 percent). Their findings indicated that while DCNN alone cannot give a precise forecast, with the aid of physicians, they were able to achieve 100% accuracy. As a result, DCNNs cannot substitute human pathology interpretations outside of tongue lesions. [74]

Jaw tumors were diagnosed using CNN in a study by Poedjiastoeti et al. The information was gathered retrospectively at a university hospital. On panoramic digital X-ray pictures, there were 250 ameloblastomas and 250 Kerato Cystic Odontogenic Tumor lesions with known biopsy results. There were 200 ameloblastoma pictures and 200 Kerato Cystic Odontogenic Tumor images in the training set. 50 ameloblastoma pictures and 50 Kerato Cystic Odontogenic tumor images were used in the study. Each image was sent into the final convolutional neural network once it had been trained. The likelihood of ameloblastoma or Kerato Cystic Odontogenic tumor per panoramic radiography picture was classified into two categories in this investigation. [75]

Lymph node metastasis in patients with oral cancer was diagnosed with a deep learning image classifier designed by Ariji Y et al. CT scans of 127 histologically confirmed positive cervical lymph nodes and 314 histologically proven negative lymph nodes from 45 patients with oral squamous cell carcinoma were utilized to evaluate the imaging data in this investigation. The Mann-Whitney U test and the Chi-square test were used to compare the diagnostic performance of deep learning with that of the two radiologists. Their findings indicated that the deep-learning image classification system performed well, with 81.0 percent specificity, 78.2 percent accuracy, 75.4 percent sensitivity, and 0.80 area under the receiver operating characteristic curve, the deep learning, and radiologists performed similarly. [76]

In a study by Hiraiwa et al, Root morphology of the mandibular first molar in panoramic radiograph was examined with deep learning diagnostic performance classification system. CBCT scans and panoramic radiographs of 760 mandibular first molars from 400 individuals who had not had root canal procedures were examined in this research. On CBCT images, distal roots were evaluated for the existence of a single or additional root. Image patches of the roots segmented from panoramic radiographs were used to test the deep learning system's diagnostic performance in the categorization of root morphology. The additional roots were found in 21.4 percent of distal roots on CBCT images, and the diagnostic accuracy of the deep learning system for determining whether distal roots were single or had extra roots was 86.9%. They determined that the deep learning system's differential identification of the additional root was highly accurate. [77]

Periapical pathosis with cone-beam computed tomography (CBCT) images assessed using DCNN was implemented by Orhan K et al. Images of 153 periapical lesions from 109 individuals were utilized. The human observer and the deep learning system were used to compare these photos. A human observer determined the precise area of the jaw and teeth linked with the periapical lesions, and these lesion volumes were computed using manual segmentation methods utilizing Fujifilm Synapse 3D software. The Wilcoxon signed-rank test and Bland–Altman analysis were used to evaluate the AI-based system identification of the lesion, specific region of the lesion, and lesion volume by (Diagnocat Inc., San Francisco, CA, USA) with the manual segmentation. According to their findings, the AI system was able to detect 142 of the 153 periapical lesions. The results were 92.8 percent reliable, which is equivalent to the manual segmentation approach, the AI-based method detected periapical pathosis was accurate.[78]

II. ARTIFICIAL INTELLIGENCE IN ORAL AND MAXILLOFACIAL SURGERY

According to American Dental Association(ADA), Oral and maxillofacial surgery is the specialty of dentistry which includes the diagnosis, surgical and adjunctive treatment of diseases, injuries, and defects involving both the functional and esthetic aspects of the hard and soft tissues of the oral and maxillofacial region. AI in the field of oral and maxillofacial surgery aids the surgeons in various aspects. These AI technologies could help in all aspects of surgery from treatment planning for surgery to postoperative complications. AI technologies could predict the prognosis of the surgery. AI is used in obtaining the reasons for extraction,

Computer-aided surgery with robotics, 3D enhanced with AI for treatment planning and to predict nodal metastasis.

Based on literature report, reasons for extraction were identified using the AI-based algorithm from digital dental records of 10582 patients, entered in the period from January 2008 to April 2010 which was taken from 5 dental clinics. After adjusting the dataset format to the appropriate processing conditions, Data Mining Server was used to execute inductive OLAP analysis on a representative sample of 250 rows. Their findings indicated that gender, age, and employment had a statistically significant influence on the proportion of patients having at least one extraction, according to AI-specific algorithms for a valuable tool for patient triage. [79]

In a review study published in 2018, Cheng F et al discussed image guiding and surgical robots in Computer-Aided Surgery [CAS]. Surgeons can obtain sufficient lesion information using image analysis and guidance in CAS to accomplish precision diagnosis and surgical planning. This allows surgeons to see anatomical features more clearly and eliminates the difficulty of hand-eye coordination. Information-driven surgical robots allow surgeons to deliver the best possible care to their patients, therefore improving treatment efficacy. [80]

Postoperative facial swelling following the impacted mandibular third molars extraction was evaluated by ANN in a study by Zhang W et al . Data from 400 patients in the hospital who had their impacted mandibular third molars extracted were randomly selected, and the neural networks model was trained and evaluated with a training sample of 300 patients and a test sample of 100 patients. Their findings indicated that the model could accurately predict facial oedema after impacted mandibular third tooth extraction. [81]

Bouletreau P et al commented on Digital solutions in orthognathic surgery which were created solely for the examination of digital models of dental arches and radiographic images. The following are some of the effects of digital solutions on surgical-orthodontic protocols: improved therapeutic follow-up due to finer interval comparison of results using image superimposing; improved diagnostic precision using AI-enhanced maxillofacial imagery; treatment planning using 3D models; CAD/CAM (Computer Aid Design, Computer Aid Manufacturing) manufacture of custom orthodontic and surgical appliances and equipment; CAD/CAM (Computer Aid Design, Computer Aid Manufacturing) manufacture of custom orthodontic and surgical appliances and equipment; they found that AI is a strong tool that may help in diagnosis, therapy, and follow-up. [82]

The main difficulties in many low and middle-income nations, according to Reddy CL et al., are operational, management, and process challenges, which reflect flaws in the surgical system rather than bad clinician decision making. AI technologies would make these inefficient procedures more efficient. All countries, especially low- and middle-income ones, have extensive data sets on surgery that will aid in the use of AI in surgery. [83]

AI aided in surgical decision-making and its outcome in a study conducted by Neuhaus M et al. In a research, 80 percent of 360 orbital CT images were utilized to train Deep Learning Classifier Networks to detect morphology and fracture features. This included trauma pre-, post-, and follow-ups, as well as non-traumatized orbits. For validation, 20% of scans (all preoperative trauma) were utilized to determine AI accuracy, which was then compared to real results. Their findings indicated that both AI and human specialists made incorrect classifications and forecasts. They concluded that AI can be a useful and accurate tool for providing analysis and predicting results in ocular trauma surgery. [84]

An artificial intelligent model for surgery/non-surgery decision and extraction determination was developed and their performance was evaluated by Choi et al. There were 316 patients in total in this research, 160 of whom were scheduled for surgical treatment and 156 of whom were scheduled for non-surgical therapy. The artificial neural network's input values were derived from 12 lateral cephalogram measurement data and six extra indices. The learning was done in three steps, with four of the best-performing models being used. The success rate was measured by comparing the real diagnosis to the artificial intelligence model's diagnosis. For the diagnosis of surgery/non-surgery decision, the model had a success rate of 96 percent, and 91 percent for the comprehensive diagnostic of operation type and extraction decision. [85]

Bur M et al in a study used Machine learning to predict occult nodal metastasis in early oral squamous cell carcinoma and compared it with the Depth of Invasion model [DOI]. In research, algorithms were developed using 782 patients from the National Cancer Database [NCDB] and validated using data from 71 patients treated at a single academic institution and employed five clinical and pathologic characteristics to predict the existence of occult lymph node metastases. Delong's test was used to evaluate the performance of the DOI model and machine learning for two associated ROC curves. In comparison to DOI, machine learning lowered the number of neck dissections suggested while increasing sensitivity and specificity. [86]

III. ARTIFICIAL INTELLIGENCE IN ORTHODONTICS

According to ADA, Orthodontics and dentofacial orthopedics is the dental specialty that includes the diagnosis, prevention, interception, and correction of malocclusion, as well as neuromuscular and skeletal abnormalities of the developing or mature orofacial structures. AI in orthodontics has been used as a decision support system, for cephalometric analysis, treatment planning, and robot-assisted archwire bending.

ANN model was developed by Xiaoqui et al to identify the need for extraction before the orthodontic treatment. The decision-making expert for the patient's orthodontic requirements in this study had a total of 200 patients ranging in age from 11 to 15 years old were selected for the research. 180 patients were utilized for ANN training, and 20 patients were tested. The results showed that the data in the testing set was 80 percent correct. The ANN model worked well as a decision expert. [87]

In 2012, Zhang Y et al investigated and tested a robotic system for archwire bending. This work presented a new robotic method for bending archwire into the required shape. Control points of end-effectors and control angles of each control point were used to create a coordinated robotic system. The robotic device was used to experiment with preliminary orthodontic wire bending. Their findings indicated that the robotic system for orthodontic wire bending may meet the practicality of the created orthodontic wire production plan. (88)

Takada K et al assessed permanent tooth extraction for orthodontic purposes using AI. Twelve cephalometric variables and six extra indices were gathered from 156 orthodontic patients for this study. 96 patients were chosen for the learning data set and 60 for the test data set, out of a total of 156. The success rate of models was 93 percent for extraction vs. non-extraction diagnosis and 84 percent for detailed extraction pattern diagnosis, according to their findings. They highlighted the fact that using a neural network machine learning AI expert system, orthodontic performance may be enhanced [89]

The orthodontic Clinical Decision Support System was created to aid general practitioners by Thanathorwong et al.

The Bayesian network (BN) was employed as a model in this study, and it was trained using the words orthodontic treatment demand and its variables collected from the publications. The findings of 1000 patient data sets from the hospital record system were compared to the opinions of two orthodontists. Their findings revealed that two orthodontists and the clinical decision support system had a high level of agreement, utilising the BN to categorize patients was extremely accurate. [90]

Kunz F et al evaluated a specialized AI algorithm for the automated cephalometric X-ray analysis and compared their accuracy with the human experts. In this research project, 12 experienced examiners identified 18 landmarks from 1792 cephalometric X-rays that were used to train the network, and the quality of the AI's predictions was evaluated. Both the AI and each examiner analyzed 12 commonly used orthodontic parameters based on 50 cephalometric X-rays. Their findings indicated that there were practically no statistically significant discrepancies between the gold standard used by humans and the predictions made by AI, they interpreted unfamiliar cephalometric X-rays with almost the same degree of accuracy as experienced human examiners. [91]

In a study by Kok H et al, the stages of the cervical vertebrae stages were identified with the seven AI classifiers. This research consisted of 300 participants aged 8 to 17 years old, 19 reference locations, and 20 distinct linear measures. k-nearest neighbors (k-NN), Naive Bayes (NB), decision tree (Tree), artificial neural networks (ANN), support vector machine (SVM), random forest (RF), and logistic regression (Log.Regr.) techniques are the seven algorithms. Artificial intelligence algorithms were used to process the measurement data, and the predicted CVS were compared to the actual CVS. In comparison to the other six algorithms, they found that ANN may be the superior approach for determining CVS. [92]

In 2019, Patcas R et al used artificial intelligence to assess the influence of orthognathic therapy on facial beauty and predicted age. Pre- and post-treatment photos of 146 orthognathic patients were obtained for this investigation. The study utilized CNN to train on more than 0.5 million pictures for age estimate and more than 17 million judgments for beauty. Their findings indicated that overallook improved after treatment (66.4%), resulting in a nearly one-year younger appearance and a 74.7 percent increase in attractiveness. AI was able to assess face beauty and apparent age in orthognathic patients. [93]

An automated orthodontic diagnostic system was created using natural language processing by Kajiwara T et al. In their investigation, 990 data sets were used, which are certifications from dentists. They were separated into 810 training data sets, 90 validation data sets, and 90 assessment data sets at random. Bag of Words [BoW], Universal Sentence Enhancer [USE], and OoK were used to transform the sentence (One-of-K). Their findings revealed that for the task of extracting orthodontic problems, they achieved a 0.585 F1-score, and for the treatment prioritization task, they achieved a 0.584 correlation coefficient with the human ranking and concluded that natural language processing aids in the development of an automated orthodontic diagnostic system. [94]

Dharmasena et al predicted the cessation of orthodontic treatments using a classification-based approach. The training data set included 310 records of clinical treatments for dental malocclusion from the Division of Orthodontics, University Dental Hospital, Peradeniya, Sri Lanka. Actual clinical data was utilized to create multiple prediction models utilizing various learning algorithms, including Nave Bayes, Random Forest, Logistic Regression, and Probit model, and the accuracy and reliability of each model were compared. The duration of therapy is the most important component in the prediction model, and the current predictive technique produced reliable findings. [95]

IV. ARTIFICIAL INTELLIGENCE IN PERIODONTICS

According to ADA, periodontics is that specialty of dentistry that encompasses the prevention, diagnosis, and treatment of diseases of the supporting and surrounding tissues of the teeth or their substitutes and the maintenance of the health, function, and esthetics of these structures and tissues. There are a group of diseases that occur in the periodontium. These diseases and their risk factors can be predicted by the AI algorithm.

Assessment of periodontitis using ANN was studied by Shankarpillai et al. A total of 230 people were evaluated for major and minor periodontitis risk factors, with grades ranging from 1 to 5. In this study, the Levenberg Marquardt method and the Scaled Conjugate Gradient algorithm were evaluated for efficacy. Their findings indicated that the Levenberg Marquardt method outperformed the Scaled Conjugate Gradient approach in both training and simulation phases, converging quicker with fewer iterations and producing the lowest mean square error. They came to the conclusion that the Levenberg Marquardt backpropagation algorithm was successful in predicting periodontitis risk. [96]

Nakano Y et al classified oral malodor from oral microbiota in saliva by using a support vector machine (SVM), ANN, and a decision tree. Using a support vector machine (SVM), an artificial neural network (ANN), and a decision tree, an efficient approach for identifying oral malodor from oral microbiota in saliva was designed. They employed peak areas of terminal restriction fragment (T-RF) length polymorphisms (T-RFLPs) of the 16S rRNA gene as data for supervised machine-learning techniques, and amounts of methyl mercaptan in mouth air as an indication of oral malodor. The 16S rRNA genes were amplified from saliva samples from 309 individuals, and the DNA fragments were subjected to T-RFLP analysis. Based on these two frequencies in 308 samples, the system was trained to classify the presence or absence of methyl mercaptan in oral air. supervised machine learning was used to classify 1 sample using the other 308 examples as training. Models to classify the presence of methyl mercaptan, a volatile sulfur-containing molecule that produces oral malodor, were constructed using T-RF proportions and frequencies, and

SVM classifiers were successful, according to their findings. (97)

The decision tree (DT), SVM, and ANN were used to create an identification unit for periodontal disease categorization by Ozden FO et al. A total of 150 patients were used in this investigation, and they were split into two groups: training (100) and testing (50). Periodontal data, risk variables, and radiographic bone loss were used as input codes in a matrix structure. The categorization unit produced six periodontal conditions in total. The recommended approaches were compared in terms of accuracy, working time, and resolution. In comparison to ANN, their findings indicated that SVM and DT had excellent accuracy. They concluded that SVM and DT can be utilized to predict periodontal diseases. (98)

In a study by Thakur A et al, Gum diseases were predicted by the Neural network. They predicted periodontal diseases using the symptoms and risk factors given by the patients. The symptom and risk factor information obtained from 200 patients with 11 attributes were the input data and were trained with the Levenberg Marquardt algorithm. The output is predicted as periodontal or gum disease. Their results revealed that the Levenberg Marquardt algorithm has an 82% of correlation coefficient in actual and targeted output and these models are useful in the prediction of gum and periodontal diseases. (99)

Shehnaz AB et al predicted periodontal diseases by the CNN model. The CNN model correctly predicted periodontal disease. With 5 characteristics, 437 patient data sets were used. To train the CNN, these characteristics constitute periodontal disease risk factors. We utilized sample data sets with normal ranges. Their findings indicated that CNN has a 93.5714 percent accuracy rate, leading them to conclude that CNN is trustworthy. [100]

In 2018, Jahantigh F F et al did research to assess the application of AI technology for periodontal disease detection using clinical indicators. The time between 2015 and 2016 in the dentistry school was taken for this study, and clinical indices in these persons were analyzed. A training set of 160 persons and a test set of 30 people were utilized to test the Levenberg Marquardt algorithm. According to experts, the input factors were age, sex, probing pocket depth, clinical attachment loss, and plaque index. Their research showed that Levenberg-Marquardet algorithms took 6.5870 seconds to complete, and they concluded that this algorithm might be utilized to diagnose periodontal disease. [101]

Lee JH et al in a literature used a deep learning-based CNN to diagnose and forecast periodontally compromised teeth (PCT). Periapical radiographic pictures were employed in this study with a self-trained network and a pre-trained deep CNN architecture. The periapical radiographic dataset was separated into 1044 training sets, 348 validation sets, and 348 test datasets. The accuracy for predicting extraction was 73.4 percent for molars and 82.8 percent for premolars clinically identified as severe PCT utilizing 64 molars and 64 premolars, while the accuracy for diagnosing PCT was 81.0 percent for premolars and 76.7 percent for molars.

They concluded that the deep CNN algorithm was useful for diagnosing and predicting outcomes. [102]

Deep CNN detected periodontal bone loss (PBL) with panoramic dental radiographs by Krois J et al. A collection of 2001 image segments from panoramic radiographs were synthesized and the percent of PBL was assessed. A deep feed-forward CNN was trained and verified using 10-times repeated group shuffling. They compared the CNNs' performance to the subjective opinions of six dental practitioners. CNN was not statistically substantially superior to the examiners, according to their findings. [103]

Kim JE et al in a literature used deep neural network to identify four distinct types of implants. Periapical radiographs from 801 patients taken at Yonsei University Dental Hospital between 2005 and 2019 were utilized. Brnemark Mk TiUnite, Dentium Implantium, Straumann Bone Level, and Straumann Tissue Level were chosen as images for the four types of implants. To find the best pre-trained network architecture, researchers evaluated Squeeze Net, GoogLeNet, ResNet-18, MobileNet-v2, and ResNet-50. Their findings demonstrated that all five models had a test accuracy of more than 90%. They found that CNN has a good level of accuracy and can categorize the four implant fixtures even with a tiny network and a minor numbing factor. [103]

V. ARTIFICIAL INTELLIGENCE IN PROSTHODONTICS

According to ADA, Prosthodontics is the dental specialty pertaining to the diagnosis, treatment planning, rehabilitation, and maintenance of the oral function, comfort, appearance, and health of patients with clinical conditions associated with missing or deficient teeth and/or oral and maxillofacial tissues using biocompatible substitutes. There is innumerable AI algorithm such as CAD-CAM, VR simulator, color matching, and surface roughness algorithm.

For dentistry students to practice dental surgical skills in the context of a crown preparation operation, a virtual reality platform was built employing haptic feedback by Rheinmora P et al. Based on interviews with experienced dentists, important feature patterns for characterizing the quality of a procedure, such as combining tool position, tool orientation, an applied force, were identified in this study and using these features for training hidden Markov models (HMMs) monitors the students' skill. Five novices (fourth-year dental students, ages 20–22) and five experts (ages 35–45) from Thammasat University's Faculty of Dentistry were selected for assessment, and crown preparation was completed. HMMs accurately categorized all test sequences into beginner and expert groups, according to their findings. The input produced by the evaluation method was well received by experts. [105]

In 2014, Sadighpour L et al created clinical decision making utilizing an artificial neural network to facilitate maxillary implant repair for edentulous maxilla patients. A total of 47 patients were involved in this study, and their clinical data were given to two faculty prosthodontists to determine important factors for deciding the final treatment choice, and the data were coded as input. 35 case datasets were utilized in the testing, and the correctness of the results was determined using 12 fresh case datasets. According to their findings, the network accuracy for the new instances was 83.3 percent. [106]

For computer color matching in dentistry, a Genetic Algorithm + Back Propagation Neural Network (GA+BPNN) Neural Network was created by Li H et al. The color of the porcelain restoration database was created by using a crystal eye dental spectrophotometer to measure the shade of the specimen. A total of 119 data sets were processed, with the training set accounting for 75% of the data and the test set for 25%. The genetic algorithm (GA) optimized the threshold values and matching precision, according to their findings. [107]

A clinical decision support model for the particular design of removable partial dentures (RPDs) in dentistry was created by Chen Q et al in 2016. For input and output outcomes, the system was trained using normal case-based reasoning. The findings of comparing 104 randomly selected patient outputs to those picked by professionals indicated that the mean average of precision (MAP) was 0.61, indicating that the proposed clinical decision support model was effective. [108]

ANN-based deep learning was used to generate color support for maxillofacial prosthesis fabrication in a study by Mine Y et al . Using a spectrophotometer, the CIE 1976 L* a* b* color space information was measured on 52 silicone elastomer specimens of various hues. A spectrophotometer was used to assess the color of the skin between the first and second metacarpal bones of 5 healthy volunteers, 1 Asian male, and 4 Asian women, all with a mean age of 22. The pigment parameters in the output data showed the quantity of white, red, yellow, and blue compounding. Their findings indicated that when comparing genuine skin color to silicone elastomer validation, the color discrepancies were significant. [109]

With Computer-Aided Design/Computer-Aided Manufacturing (CAD/CAM) Composite Resin Crowns, CNN predicted debonding in a study by Yamaguchi et al. The study comprised CAD/CAM CR crowns made by the Division of Prosthodontics at Osaka University Dental Hospital between April 2014 and November 2015. A total of 24.8,640 photos were randomly divided into training 6,480, validation images, and testing 2,160 images in the data set, which included 12 trouble-free and 12 debonding images. For training and validation, 3,240 trouble-free and 3,240 debonding states were employed, with 1,080 trouble-free and 1,080 debonding states in the same ratio. For each epoch, the training pictures were divided into 32 batches. 100 epochs were conducted with a learning rate of 0.0001 for each epoch. A CNN was created using the Keras library (version 2.2.4) on top of Tensor Flow (GPU version

1.12.2) in Python (version 3.7.2), and it was run on a laptop computer that was connected to a graphic processing unit box (AKiTiO Node) via Thunderbolt 3 cables and had a high-performance graphics card (GeForce RTX2080: 8GB RAM; MSI). Their findings revealed that for the prediction of the debonding probability, prediction accuracy was 98.5 percent, precision was 97.0 percent, the recall was 100 percent, and F-measure values of deep learning with a CNN method for the prediction of the debonding probability were 0.985, with a mean calculation time of 2 ms/step for 2,160 test images. [110]

Deniz ST et al in a study compared the accuracy of the ANN prediction models for surface roughness and microhardness of denture teeth with the results of in vitro experiments. Vickers microhardness and surface roughness values were evaluated on maxillary molars of four distinct denture teeth after they were exposed to tea, coffee, cola, cherry juice, and distilled water. Conventional acrylic resin teeth (Major Dent, Major Prodotti, Dentari, Moncalieri, Italy), reinforced acrylic resin teeth (Integral, Merz Dental, Lütjenburg, Germany), micro filler composite resin teeth (SR Orthosit PE, Ivoclar Vivadent, Schaan, Lichtenstein), and nanofiller composite resin teeth (Veracia, Shofu, Kyoto, Japan). Each of the 5 solutions was submerged in 10 maxillary first and second molars for a total of 200 specimens from each group of denture teeth, with distilled water serving as a control. A profilometer was used to assess the average roughness (Ra) (Mahr Perthometer M2, Mahr, Germany). Three measurements were taken three times for each specimen. Experimentally collected data was utilized to train the ANN, and data from additional experimental values were used to test the trained network. According to their findings, a neural network design with one input layer of ten neurons, two hidden layers of six neurons, one output layer of two neurons, and an epoch duration of 48 provides superior prediction. [111]

Arenal AA et al in a literature constructed ANN model with the occlusal factors for prediction of bruxism. Researchers used 325 individuals, 145 of whom were diagnosed as grinding patients and 180 as clenching patients. The ANN model's input data came from measurements obtained during a patient's examination. Occlusal factors and demographic data, such as age and gender, were gathered from the patient. All variables were separately standardized to the range [0, 1] before the research was conducted. Two different skilled dentists recorded the values of all the variables. supervised learning was used to train the network, with weighted connections linking the different layers of the network being suitably chosen. The bagging method had the best predictive value of 97.2 percent for grinding patients and 89.5 percent for clenching patients, according to their findings. With only a few factors and a high probability of success, the ANN model could discriminate between clenching and grinding patients. [112]

VI. ARTIFICIAL INTELLIGENCE IN CONSERVATIVE DENTISTRY AND ENDODONTICS

According to ADA, Endodontics is the branch of dentistry that is concerned with the morphology, physiology, and pathology of the human dental pulp and periradicular tissues. Its study and practice encompass the basic and clinical sciences including biology of the normal pulp, the etiology, diagnosis, prevention, and treatment of diseases and injuries of the pulp and associated periradicular conditions. The AI algorithms in this branch of dentistry were developed on the decision support system to identify dental caries using the radiograph, clinical decision support system, predict the apical lesion, and case difficulty.

Bayesian Network[BN] was used to construct a decision-making system tool for choosing treatment strategies for dental caries in a study by Bhatia A et al. With the aid of a dentist, the conditional probability tables were calculated. BN of dental caries includes symptom nodes such as caries, cavity, fistula, swelling, food encrustation, previously broken filing, sensitivity, pain, tenderness on percussion, partial denture, pulp exposure, high filing as a sign, and treatment nodes such as RCT, relieve high points, direct pulp capping, indirect pulp capping, resolution. Their findings indicated that using BN to determine an appropriate treatment strategy for dental caries was effective.[113]

Ali R et al constructed deep neural networks to identify X-rays with dental caries. They divided dental X-ray pictures into two categories: decaying and healthy teeth. They utilized 1/3 of the photos for each class's training set, while the remaining images from the dataset were used for the test set. The input pictures were 64 by 64 pixels in size. The pixels in the pictures were modified to a value between 0 and 1. Every network has a hidden layer with three units and an output layer. Each event was repeated 20 times, with 500 iterations for training and 400 for final learning. They used the outcome of the confusion matrix to assess the quality. Their deep neural networks performed extremely well in the classification test, with a 97 percent accuracy rate. Predictions for tooth decay were right 98 percent of the time and 96.1 percent of the time for normal teeth. 96 percent of all tooth decay cases were properly predicted as decaying teeth. 98 percent of all normal teeth instances were accurately categorized. In total, 97% of the forecasts were right. Larger database would increase the accuracy and reliability of the results. [114]

Albahbah AA et al developed a novel method for detecting cavities in panoramic pictures. A total of 100 pictures were used, with the training set containing 60 images, the validation set containing 15 images, and the test data set containing 25 images. The suggested technique outperforms the ANN-based strategy, according to simulation findings. The suggested structure SVM-PSO Particle Swarm Optimization methods for classification were embedded and developed on a PC framework with specific components using Matlab 2014b x64 bit. These components were dubbed equipment, and they included an Intel Processor with a speed of 2.0 GHz and 64-bit architecture. Their research showed that training precision was 97.2 percent, validation precision was 86.7 percent, testing precision was 92.4 percent, and total precision was 92.1 percent thus employing PSO optimized SVM training showed its efficacy. [115]

Machine learning approaches were used to forecast the apical lesion of the teeth in a literature by Mahmoud YE et al. Image Preprocessing follows data gathering. 1. Eliminate Noise 2. Completed histogram, equalization, feature extraction, classification, and assessment. 201 datasets of dental x-ray pictures for teeth periapical lesion were acquired for the dentistry hospital at MSA University in Egypt. The data was first split into four categories: APA (Acute Periapical Abscess), AAP (Acute Apical Periodontitis), CPA (Chronic Periapical Abscess), and Normal. They are then divided into infected and non-infected groups. The photos were converted from hard copies to soft copies using a camera with a 7.2 Mega-Pixel CCD that captures enough information for photo-quality 15 x 20-inch prints, producing images 30722304 in JPEG format. 2D discrete wavelet transformations that yielded picture sub-band images (H1, V1, D1, H2, V2, D2, and A2). To construct the feature vector, several estimators may be generated for these sub-bands. V1 and V2, D1 and D2, V1, V2, D1, D2, and A2 – [KNN] K-Nearest Neighbor Classifier 78.26 percent, 78.26 percent, 82.61 percent, and Feed Forward NN 52.17 percent, 34.78 percent, 39.13 percent, respectively. The

K-Nearest Neighbor Classifier was shown to be superior to the Feed Forward Neural Network. [116]

Yin MS et al constructed a haptic feedback to teach endodontic surgeons how to apply force correctly. Rhienmora et al. built a virtual reality dental simulator for this investigation. [112] As a dental handpiece, the simulator uses a conventional PC linked to a PHANTOM Omni haptic device. The simulator was placed in front of the participant at elbow height. For the pre-training/post-training control group design, the study included ten dental student participants (5 men and 5 females). For familiarisation, each participant was given 10 minutes. A trained endodontic teacher offered feedback to the control group on the results. Using the analysis given by the device, the teacher issued feedback to the experiment group on the quantity and direction of force put on the handpiece at each stage of the operation. Their results revealed that there were no significant variations in pre-training outcome ratings between the groups (p > 0.4). The researchers concluded that this assessment and feedback method may be a useful complement to dental physical skill training. [117]

In 2019, Fukuda M et al published research on the effectiveness of an artificial intelligence system for identifying vertical root fracture (VRF) on panoramic radiography. From 300 panoramic pictures in our hospital imaging collection, 330 VRF tooth images with clearly apparent fracture lines were chosen for this investigation. Two radiologists and one endodontist verified the VRF lines. 240 photos were allocated to the training set, accounting for 80% of the 300 total images, while 60 images were assigned to the testing set, accounting for 20% of the total images. DetectNet with DIGITS version 5.0 was used to create a CNN-based deep learning model for VRF detection, including five-fold cross-validation. Their study revealed that 267 of the 330 VRF teeth were identified, with 20 teeth without fractures being mistakenly reported. Their recall was 0.75, their accuracy was 0.93, and their F measure was 0.83. They found that employing a CNN learning model to detect VRFs on panoramic pictures and as a CAD tool, it is a promising tool. [118]

In Endodontics, a new automated technique was introduced for the precision of case complexity and referral choices in a study by Mallishery S et al. After gaining the patients' agreement, the AAE Case Difficulty Assessment Form was utilized. 500 patients who attended the dentistry school were diagnosed as requiring endodontic treatment, and the completed AAE forms were reviewed by two endodontists. An Android application was created to keep track of each completed form as well as the referral decision. The forms were able to be easily digitalized as a result of this. Android Studio (Google Inc., Mountain View, CA, USA) was used to create the app, which uses the Java programming language to create apps for the Android platform.

The data and training sets were chosen at random and fed into the machine learning algorithm. They were used to train the support vector machine (SVM) and deep neural network (DNN). Their findings indicated that SVM-data-raw 94.80, SVM-data-summarized 92.60, DNN-data-raw

93.40, DNN-data-summarized 92.20, and Actual not referred 242 referred 258, SVM-data-summarized not referred- 247, referred -253, DNN-data-raw did not refer -245, referred- 255, DNN-data-summarized not referred -25, by anticipating the complexity level of a case, they may offer an alternative to the traditional technique that is more automated.[119]

VII. ARTIFICIAL INTELLIGENCE IN PEDODONTICS

According to ADA, pediatric dentistry is an age-defined specialty that provides both primary and comprehensive preventive and therapeutic oral health care for infants and children through adolescence, including those with special health care needs. AI can be utilized in various areas of this specialty.

In 2012, Moghimi S et al. published research in which they developed a (GA–ANN) system and a unique hybrid genetic algorithm to estimate the sizes of unerupted canines and premolars throughout the mixed dentition phase. 106 untreated participants (52 girls and 54 boys) aged 13–15 years were involved in this study, and their data was gathered through tooth cast measurements. A hybrid GA–ANN method was used to find the best reference teeth and the most accurate mapping function. Based on regression analysis, the greatest connection was found between the total of the mandibular canines and premolars and the mesiodistal widths of the mandibular first molars and incisors (r = 0.697). The total of the mesiodistal widths of the canines and premolars and the mesiodistal widths of the mandibular first molars and maxillary central incisors had the strongest connection in the maxilla (0.742). The GA – ANN used the mandibular first molars and incisors, as well as the maxillary central incisors, as reference teeth for estimating the sum of the canine and premolar mesiodistal widths. The maximum rates of over/underestimation and prediction error rates. They found that the (GA–ANN) system and a unique hybrid genetic algorithm may accurately estimate the size of unerupted premolars and canines throughout the mixed dentition phase. [120]

An ANN model was created for the prediction of post-streptococcus mutans in dental caries in a study by Javed S et al. 45 primary molar tooth cases were investigated in this study, which focused on occlusal dentinal caries in children. Polymer burs, carbide burs, and spoon excavators were used to excavate caries. The colony-forming units of pre-and post-Streptococcus mutans were recorded, and ANN models based on clinical trial data were used. With the recorded clinical data, ANN models were trained, verified, and tested using various architectures. Their findings indicated that a feedforward backpropagation ANN model with an architecture of 4-5-1 predicted post-Streptococcus mutans with an efficiency of 0.99033, mean squared error and mean absolute percentage, and error for testing cases was 0.2341 and 4.967, respectively. The caries excavation methods and pre-Streptococcus mutans served as input feeds, with post-Streptococcus mutans serving as goals for developing the ANN model. The iOS App was created to assist in the decision-making process when choosing a caries excavation method. The App may be used by a global physician to accurately forecast post-Streptococcus mutans on iPhone based on pre-Streptococcus mutans. [121]

You W et al in a study used a deep learning-based approach to identify dental plaque on primary teeth and compared it to clinical evaluation. The CNN framework was employed in this investigation, and 886 intraoral images of primary teeth were used for training. The AI model was used to evaluate 98 intraoral images of primary teeth to confirm clinical feasibility. A digital camera was also used to take photographs of the teeth. One expert pediatric dentist reviewed the pictures and noted plaque-containing areas. The plaque was then recognized with the use of a plaque disclosing agent. After a week, the dentist re-drew the plaque area on the 98 images obtained by the digital camera to evaluate it. According to their findings, for identifying plaque on the tested dental images, the MIoU 0.726 0.165 was used. When Dentists initially diagnosed the 98 images shot by the digital camera, the MIoU was 0.695 0.269, and after one week, it was 0.689 0.253. In comparison to the dentist, the AI model had a higher MIoU (0.736 0.174), and the results did not alter after one week. When the dentist and the AI model analyzed the 102 intraoral images, the MIoU was 0.652 0.195 for the dentist and 0.724 0.159 for the model. In the paired t-test, there was no significant difference between the human specialist and the AI model in identifying dental plaque on main teeth (P >.05) with that p was clinically acceptable. [122]

VIII. ARTIFICIAL INTELLIGENCE IN PUBLIC HEALTH DENTISTRY

According to ADA, Dental public health is the science and art of preventing and controlling dental diseases and promoting dental health through organized community efforts. It is that form of dental practice which serves the community as a patient rather than the individual. It is concerned with the dental health education of the public, with applied dental research, and with the administration of group dental care programs as well as the prevention and control of dental diseases on a community basis. The use of an AI system could be done in numerous ways that aids the researcher.

In 2009, Tamaki Y et al conducted a study that used data mining to create a dental caries prediction model. This research included 560 children from the Ena and Nakatsugawa regions of Gifu Prefecture, Japan, who were a sample population of pre-elementary pupils. Fluoride levels in drinking water should not exceed 0.08 parts per million. 500 youngsters between the ages of 5 and 8 were monitored for three years. Salivary pH, Streptococci mutans and lactobacilli, 3 min stimulated saliva volume, fluoride use, and frequency of beverage and snack consumption were all included as factors. Among the 30 schools, 13 primary schools were chosen as a sample. Their parents received a letter informing them about the study. After 2.5 years, 48 children had fallen out of follow-up. The decaying, filled tooth was recorded using the standard WHO technique and criteria for the clinical assessment. Saliva samples were obtained after chewing gum was used to stimulate saliva, and microbiological treatments were performed thereafter. Initially, traditional models based on logistic regression analysis, decision analysis, and neural networks were employed, followed by novel models based on randomly chosen individuals with the same number and no new dental caries. For each approach, ten models were created. [123]

IX. ARTIFICIAL INTELLIGENCE IN ORAL AND MAXILLOFACIAL PATHOLOGY AND FORENSIC ODONTOLOGY

According to ADA, Oral pathology is the specialty of dentistry and discipline of pathology that deals with the nature, identification, and management of diseases affecting the oral and maxillofacial regions. It is a science that investigates the causes, processes, and effects of these diseases. The practice of oral pathology includes research and diagnosis of diseases using clinical, radiographic, microscopic, biochemical, or other examinations. AI can be most utilized by Oral pathologists in order to rectify the improper diagnosis due to fatigue.

Boora RC et al in a study created an open case-based decision-support system for diagnosis in oral pathology. An alternate tool for aiding dentistry students in overcoming the challenging oral pathology learning process The C++ programming language was used to create a Bayes theorem based on a decision-support system connected to a relational database. After the system was trained using data from 401 cases of oral bone disease, the simulation was run. They are then tested by diagnosing 43 known instances of oral bone disease using software developed for the computerization of a surgical pathology service and simulation. [124]

Chang SW et al conducted a study using a hybrid of feature selection and machine learning methods for the oral cancer prognosis based on clinicopathologic and genomic markers. Machine learning techniques were used as they are good for handling noisy and incomplete data, and significant results can be attained despite a small sample size. A total of 31 oral cancer cases from 2003 to 2007 were selected from the Malaysian Oral Cancer Database and Tissue Bank System (MOCDTBS) coordinated by OCRCC, Faculty of Dentistry, University of Malaya. Four classification methods are used for testing and comparing from both machine learning and statistical methods. They found the best feature selection method for oral cancer prognosis was ReliefF-GA with ANFIS classification. [125]

For early diagnosis and prevention of oral cancer, a data mining model based on probabilistic neural networks and general regression neural networks (PNN/GRNN) was developed by Sharma N et al. All of the datasets from the oral cancer registries were included. The model was built using 35 attributes and 1025 records of the oral cancer database. All clinical symptoms and history are evaluated in the categorization of malignant and non-malignant cases, and it also forecasts a specific kind of cancer, its extent, and stage with the assistance of symptoms, gross examination, and investigations such as histology reports. [126]

Oral exfoliative cytology was used in a study by Chatterjee S et al to suggest a computer-assisted technique for diagnosing oral pre-cancer/cancer. The researchers integrated numerous retrieved characteristics from cytology of individuals with oral submucous fibrosis, oral leukoplakia, or oral squamous cell carcinoma (OSCC) and those with no disease. Predictive machine learning models such as the random forest, k closest neighbour, and support vector machine were trained using these features. They stated that the verification experiments showed to be having a test accuracy of over 90%. [127]

Multiplayer Perceptron Neural Networks (MLPNN) and image processing techniques were constructed to detect gender and age from dental x-ray pictures in a study by Avuclu et al. The innovative method was used to make high-level predictions and to achieve certain outcomes. At first, the image pre-processing techniques were used on pictures of teeth. They used pre-processing techniques to apply to pictures of teeth. Following the, a new segmentation technique was used to segment the tooth pictures to extract the feature. The teeth are dynamically and automatically segmented. The numerical data acquired from feature extraction from dental pictures were fed into a Multi-layer perceptron neural network as inputs. The program may do the feature reduction. The greatest categorization success rates were 99.9% (full segment) and 100 percent (not complete segment). After numerous classifications, the dental group's age estimate is done with 0% error. With the application, an interdisciplinary study was created. The picture dataset in this study is made up of a training set of photos kept in a separate folder and a testing set of images stored in other files, which are then utilized as the database following MPLNN training. The picture was segmented using binary segmentation. The segmentation process was fluid and could be broken down into any size. The Average Absolute Deviation (AAD) technique was used to extract features for each partition, which were divided by segments. A total of 1315 pictures of teeth were utilized as the study's database. For the database, 162 distinct tooth classifications were manually generated. The algorithm for determining age and gender was developed, trained, and tested. They concluded that MLPNN was categorized as having the greatest accuracy rate of 100 percent and that a gender determination process was also carried out. [128]

For age estimate, a CNN-based examination of dental images was built in a study by Alkaabi et al. They used dental panoramic X-ray images to test several Convolutional Neural Network (CNN) architectures for age estimate. More than 2000 X-ray pictures were utilized to train the CNN architectures in the training dataset, which was split into seven groups. The popular CNN architectures were trained using transfer learning concepts such as AlexNet, VGGNet, and ResNet for age estimation. For all of the architectures that were tested, the recall, precision, F1-score, accuracies, and average accuracies were used to evaluate the performance of the age estimate. The custom dataset 2575 panoramic X-ray pictures were utilized in this study to evaluate all of the structures, and the photos were split into seven age groups: 10, 10-19, 20-29, 30-39, 40-49, 50-60, and 60+. The distribution of training and test data sets was done at random. The original size of the pictures was 1991 x 1127, however, they were reduced to fit the network topologies utilized. Before using CNN, all of the pictures were normalized. The accuracy of age estimation was enhanced with CNN design. [129]

In a 2019 study, Farhadian M et al used the pulp-to-tooth ratio in canines to estimate dental age using neural networks. For the investigation, they employed archived cone-beam computed tomographic (CBCT) images from 300 patients. The results revealed that the neural network model outperformed the regression model in terms of age estimation. In a forensic study, the neural network models provided better accurate age predictions than a linear regression model. [130]

A comprehensive categorization model for estimating Dental Age (DA) in Indian children was designed by Hemalatha B et al. For the categorization of DA, the Fuzzy Neural Network with Teaching Learning-Based Optimization (FNN-TLBO) was developed. An orthopantomogram (OPG) was used to assess the dental age and chronological age of about 100 healthy, south Indian children and adolescents aged 4–18 years. Their analysis shows that TLBO outperforms current algorithms such as the Modified Extreme Learning Machine with Sparse Representation Classification (MELM-SRC) and the Adaptive Neuro-Fuzzy Inference System in terms of deference execution (ANFIS). [131]

Patil V et al constructed an artificial neural network for gender determination using mandibular morphometric data. For gender determination, this study employed Artificial Neural Networks (ANN) and compared the findings with logistic regression and discriminant analysis utilizing mandibular characteristics as inputs. The mandible was measured using digital panoramic radiographs from 509 people. Each individual's 6 linear parameters and 1 angular parameter were collected. This was six-month retrospective research that was done after receiving clearance from the institutional ethical committee. 1000 digital panoramic radiographs were chosen from the existing database, which was obtained with a Kodak 8000C Digital Panoramic and Cephalometric system with exposure values of 66kVp, 12mA, and 14s. They are categorized into 444 for training, 95 for testing, and 95 for validation based on their parameter combinations. They determined that the parameters were subjected to Logistic Regression, Discriminant Analysis, and ANN analysis, with ANN having a greater accuracy of 75 percent, discriminant analysis having an overall accuracy of 69.1 percent, and logistic regression having an accuracy of 69.9 percent. ANN has shown to be a predictive tool that may be used in the field of forensic sciences to provide near-perfect predictions. [132]

ARTIFICIAL INTELLIGENCE SOFTWARE

1. IBM Watson.
2. Engati.
3. Deep Vision.
4. Cloud Machine Learning Engine.
5. Salesforce Einstein.
6. Azure Machine Learning Studio.
7. TensorFlow.
8. Infosys Nia.
9. H2O AI
10. CORTANA.[133]
11. Amazon Alexa
12. Google Assistant.

Azure Machine Learning Studio, TensorFlow, H2O AI, IBM Watson, Amazon Alexa, Google Assistant are free softwares

Epilogue

Artificial intelligence is progressively being employed in everyday life in this modern era, and its application in dentistry is emerging. There is an enormous amount of information available in healthcare that may be used to train various ANN models to assist dentists in evaluating the patient. These ANN models will not replace healthcare experts; rather, they will assist in the accurate diagnosis and/or treatment of patients based on models developed by healthcare professionals. These models could be designed for use in dentistry.

TABLE 1:

SL.NO	TYPE OF AI	LOGIC	STUDIES
1.	i)Machine Learning ii)Artificial Neural network iii)Convolutional Neural Network	Large data is required for the training of algorithm	Detection of apical pathosis Determination of gender using OPG For age estimation
2.	Fuzzy logic	Yes or no/ true or false	Detect change in color of the tooth after bleaching

3.	Rule based expert system	Educating students	Visual expert for identification of ulcer and determining the need for extraction in orthodontic treatment
4.	Physical robots	Pre- defined tasks	Computer-Assisted Surgical Planning and Robotics (CASPAR)
5.	Robotic process automation	Automation with help of computer	Computer Aided Surgery

TABLE 2: ABBREVIATIONS

ADA	-	American dental association
AI	-	Artificial intelligence
ALICE	-	Artificial linguistic internet computer entity
ANN	-	Artificial neural network
BN	-	Bayesian network
CAD CAM	-	Computer aided design computer aided machine
CAS	-	Computer aided surgery
CASPAR	-	Computer aided surgical planning and robotics
CBCT	-	Cone beam computed tomography
CDSS	-	Clinical decision support system

CNN	-	Convolutional neural network
DNN	-	Deep neural network
FNN	-	Fuzzy neural network
GA	-	Genetic algorithm
GDSS	-	Group decision support system
GRNN	-	General regression neural network
ML	-	Machine learning
MLP	-	Multilayer perceptron
NLP	-	Natural language processing
NN	-	Neural network
OPML	-	Oral premalignant lesion
OSCC	-	Oral squamous cell carcinoma
PNN	-	Probabilistic neural network
RF	-	Random forest
SVM	-	Support vector machine
XCON	-	Expert configurer

References

1. Ahuja AS. The impact of artificial intelligence in medicine on the future role of the physician. PeerJ. 2019 Oct 4;7:e7702.
2. Wang F, Preininger A. AI in Health: State of the Art, Challenges, and Future Directions. Yearbook of medical informatics. 2019 Aug;28(01):016-26.
3. Davenport T, Kalakota R. The potential for artificial intelligence in healthcare. Future healthcare journal. 2019 Jun;6(2):94.
4. Park WJ, Park JB. History and application of artificial neural networks in dentistry. European journal of dentistry. 2018 Oct;12(04):594-601.
5. Jiang F, Jiang Y, Zhi H, Dong Y, Li H, Ma S, Wang Y, Dong Q, Shen H, Wang Y. Artificial intelligence in healthcare: past, present, and future. Stroke and vascular neurology. 2017 Dec 1;2(4):230-43.
6. Zhang J, Song Y, Xia F, Zhu C, Zhang Y, Song W, Xu J, Ma X. Rapid and accurate intraoperative pathological diagnosis by artificial intelligence with deep learning technology. Medical hypotheses. 2017 Sep 1;107:98-9.
7. Palma SI, Traguedo AP, Porteira AR, Frias MJ, Gamboa H, Roque AC. Machine learning for the meta-analyses of microbial pathogens' volatile signatures. Scientific reports. 2018 Feb 20;8(1):1-5.
8. Majumdar B, Sarode SC, Sarode GS, Patil S. Technology: artificial intelligence. British dental journal. 2018 Jun;224(12):916.
9. Hung K, Montalvao C, Tanaka R, Kawai T, Bornstein MM. The use and performance of artificial intelligence applications in dental and maxillofacial radiology: A systematic review. Dentomaxillofacial Radiology. 2020 Jan;49(1):20190107.
10. Mintz Y, Brodie R. Introduction to artificial intelligence icn medicine. Minimally Invasive Therapy & Allied Technologies. 2019 Mar 4;28(2):73-81.
11. Nilsson NJ. The quest for artificial intelligence. Cambridge University Press;2009 Oct 30.12. Perlovsky LI. Neural mechanisms of the mind, Aristotle, Zadeh, and MRI. IEEE Transactions on Neural Networks. 2010 Mar 1;21(5):718-33.

13. A. M. Turing, Computing Machinery and Intelligence, 1950. Mind 49: 433-460.

14. Kline R. Cybernetics, automata studies, and the Dartmouth conference on artificial intelligence. IEEE Annals of the History of Computing. 2010 Jun 3;33(4):5-16.

15. McCulloch WS, Pitts W. A logical calculus of the ideas immanent in nervous activity. The bulletin of mathematical biophysics. 1943 Dec 1;5(4):115-33.

16. Poulton MM. A Brief History. Oxford: Elsevier Science; 2001: p. 10

17. Gugerty L. Newell and Simon's logic theorist: historical background and impact on cognitive modeling. InProceedings of the Human Factors and Ergonomics Society Annual Meeting 2006 Oct;50 (9):880-884.

18. Munoz A. Machine Learning and Optimization in Courant Institute of Mathematical Sciences, New York. NY.URL: https://www. cims. nyu. edu/~munoz/files/ml_optimization. pdf [accessed 2016-03-02] [WebCite Cache ID 6fiLfZvnG]. 2014.

19. Dreyfus HL, Hubert L. What computers still can't do: A critique of artificial reason. MIT press; 1992.

20. Natale S. If software is narrative: Joseph Weizenbaum, artificial intelligence and the biographies of ELIZA. new media & society. 2019 Mar;21(3):712-28.

21. Weizenbaum J. ELIZA—a computer program for the study of natural language communication between man and machine. Communications of the ACM. 1966 Jan 1;9(1):36-45.

22. Ho Y, Bryson A, Baron S. Differential games and optimal pursuit-evasion strategies. IEEE Transactions on Automatic Control. 1965 Oct;10(4):385-9.

23. Bryson A, Ho Y. Applied Optimal Control: Optimization, Estimation, and control. New York: Taylor and Francis; 1975.

24. Jackson P. Introduction to expert systems. Addison-Wesley Longman Publishing Co., Inc.; 1998 Dec 1.

25. Dudhrejia MH, Shah MS. Speech Recognition using Neural Networks.2018 Oct;7(10):196-202.

26. Bachant J, McDermott J. R1 revisited: Four years in the trenches. AI Magazine. 1984 Sep 15;5(3):21-21.

27. Kato I, Ohteru S, Kobayashi H, Shirai K, Uchiyama A. Information-Power Machine with Senses and Limbs (WABOT-1) First CISM - IFToMM Symp Theory Pract Robot Manip. 1974;1:11–24.

28. Rosheim ME. Robot evolution: the development of anthrobotics. John Wiley & Sons; 1994 Aug 11.

29. Konno A, Nagashima K, Furukawa R, Nishiwaki K, Noda T, Inaba M, Inoue H. Development of a humanoid robot Saika. InProceedings of the 1997 IEEE/RSJ International Conference on Intelligent Robot and Systems. Innovative Robotics for Real-World Applications. IROS'97 1997 Sep 11 ;2: 805-810.

30. Sakagami Y, Watanabe R, Aoyama C, Matsunaga S, Higaki N, Fujimura K. The intelligent ASIMO: System overview and integration. In IEEE/ RSJ international conference on intelligent robots and systems 2002 Oct;3:2478-2483.

31. Siegel M, Breazeal C, Norton MI. Persuasive robotics: The influence of robot gender on human behavior. In2009 IEEE/RSJ International Conference on Intelligent Robots and Systems 2009 Oct 10 .2563-2568.

32. Ceccarelli M, editor. Technology Developments: the Role of Mechanism and Machine Science and IFToMM. Springer Science & Business Media; 2011 May 26.

33. Hirai K, Hirose M, Haikawa Y, Takenaka T. The development of Honda humanoid robot. InProceedings. 1998 IEEE International Conference on Robotics and Automation (Cat. No. 98CH36146) 1998 May 20. 2:1321-1326.

34. Shapiro EY. The fifth-generation project—a trip report. Communications of the ACM. 1983 Sep 1;26(9):637-41.

35. London S. DXplainTM: A Web-Based Diagnostic Decision Support System for Medical Students. Medical reference services quarterly. 1998 May 7;17(2):17-28.

36. Kahn MG, Steib SA, Fraser VJ, Dunagan WC. An expert system for culture-based infection control surveillance. InProceedings of the Annual Symposium on Computer Application in Medical Care 1993:171.

37. AbuShawar B, Atwell E. ALICE chatbot: trials and outputs. Computación y Sistemas. 2015 Dec;19(4):625-32.

38. Vijayarani M, Balamurugan G. Chatbot in mental health care. Indian Journal of Psychiatric Nursing. 2019 Feb 1;16(2):126.

39. Amisha PM, Pathania M, Rathaur VK. Overview of artificial intelligence in medicine. Journal of family medicine and primary care. 2019 Jul;8(7):2328.

40. Bellman R. An introduction to artificial intelligence: Can computers think?Thomson Course Technology; 1978.

41. Panch T, Szolovits P, Atun R. Artificial intelligence, machine learning, and health systems. Journal of global health. 2018 Dec;8(2).

42. Definition "Artificial Intelligence." Available from:https://www. merriamwebster.com/dictionary/artificial%20intelligence.

43. Russell, S. J. & Norvig, P. Artificial Intelligence: A Modern Approach (Prentice Hall, New Jersey, 2010).

44. Strong AI. Applications of artificial intelligence & associated technologies. Science [ETEBMS-2016]. 2016 Mar;5(6).

45. Albus JS. Outline for a theory of intelligence. IEEE transactions on systems, man, and cybernetics. 1991 May;21(3):473-509.

46. Zackova E. Intelligence explosion quest for humankind. In Beyond Artificial Intelligence Springer, Cham. 2015:(31-43).47. Mahmoud YE, Labib SS, Mokhtar HM. Teeth periapical lesion prediction using machine learning techniques. In2016 SAI Computing Conference (SAI) 2016 Jul 13 (pp. 129-134). IEEE.

48. Nadkarni PM, Ohno-Machado L, Chapman WW. Natural language processing: an introduction. Journal of the American Medical Informatics Association. 2011 Sep 1;18(5):544-51.

49. Godil SS, Shamim MS, Enam SA, Qidwai U. Fuzzy logic: A "simple" solution for complexities in neurosciences?. Surgical neurology international. 2011;2.

50. Herrera LJ, Pulgar R, Santana J, Cardona JC, Guillén A, Rojas I, del Mar Pérez M. Prediction of color change after tooth bleaching using fuzzy logic for Vita Classical shades identification. Applied Optics. 2010 Jan 20;49(3):422-9.

51. Wu S, Meng J, Yu Q, Li P, Fu S. Radiomics-based machine learning methods for isocitrate dehydrogenase genotype prediction of diffuse gliomas. Journal of cancer research and clinical oncology. 2019 Mar 13;145(3):543-50.

52. Louw DF, Fielding T, McBeth PB, Gregoris D, Newhook P, Sutherland GR. Surgical robotics: a review and neurosurgical prototype development. Neurosurgery. 2004 Mar 1;54(3):525-37.

53. Poedjiastoeti W, Suebnukarn S. Application of Convolutional Neural Network in the Diagnosis of Jaw Tumors. Healthc Inform Res. 2018 Jul;24(3):236–41.

54. LeCun Y, Bengio Y, Hinton G. Deep learning. nature. 2015 May;521(7553):436-44.

55. Ferrucci D, Brown E, Chu-Carroll J, Fan J, Gondek D, Kalyanpur AA, Lally A, Murdock JW, Nyberg E, Prager J, Schlaefer N. Building

Watson: An overview of the DeepQA project. AI Magazine. 2010 Jul 28;31(3):59-79.

56. Min H. Artificial intelligence in supply chain management: theory and applications. International Journal of Logistics: Research and Applications. 2010 Feb 1;13(1):13-39.

57. Shiwei He, Rui Song, and Sohail S. Chaudhry. Service-oriented intelligent group decision support system: Application in transportation management. Information Systems Frontiers 16, 5 November 2014: 939–951.

58. Nye BD. Intelligent tutoring systems by and for the developing world: A review of trends and approaches for educational technology in a global context. International Journal of Artificial Intelligence in Education. 2015 Jun 1;25(2):177-203.

59. Kaplan A, Haenlein M. Siri, Siri, in my hand: Who's the fairest in the land? On the interpretations, illustrations, and implications of artificial intelligence. Business Horizons. 2019 Jan 1;62(1):15-25.

60. Klimov D, Shahar Y, Taieb-Maimon M. Intelligent visualization and exploration of time-oriented data of multiple patients. Artificial intelligence in medicine. 2010 May 1;49(1):11-31.

61. Guidi G, Iadanza E, Pettenati MC, Milli M, Pavone F, Gentili GB. Heart failure artificial intelligence-based computer-aided diagnosis telecare system. In International Conference on Smart Homes and Health Telematics. Springer, Berlin, Heidelberg.2012 Jun 12:278-281.

62. Bennett CC, Hauser K. Artificial intelligence framework for simulating clinical decision-making: A Markov decision process approach. Artificial intelligence in medicine. 2013 Jan 1;57(1):9-19.

63. Gulshan V, Peng L, Coram M, Stumpe MC, Wu D, Narayanaswamy A, Venugopalan S, Widner K, Madams T, Cuadros J, Kim R. Development and validation of a deep learning algorithm for detection of diabetic retinopathy in retinal fundus photographs. Jama. 2016 Dec 13;316(22):2402-10.

64. El-Jerjawi NS, Abu-Naser SS. Diabetes Prediction Using Artificial Neural Network. International Journal of Advanced Science and Technology.2019.121:55-64.

65. Haenssle HA, Fink C, Schneiderbauer R, Toberer F, Buhl T, Blum A, Kalloo A, Hassen AB, Thomas L, Enk A, Uhlmann L. Man against the machine: diagnostic performance of a deep learning convolutional neural network for dermoscopic melanoma recognition in comparison to 58 dermatologists. Annals of Oncology. 2018 Aug 1;29(8):1836-42.

66. Somashekhar SP, Sepúlveda MJ, Puglielli S, Norden AD, Shortliffe EH, Rohit Kumar C, Rauthan A, Arun Kumar N, Patil P, Rhee K, Ramya Y. Watson for Oncology and breast cancer treatment recommendations: agreement with an expert multidisciplinary tumor board. Annals of Oncology. 2018 Feb 1;29(2):418-23.

67. Dar-Odeh NS, Alsmadi OM, Bakri F, Abu-Hammour Z, Shehabi AA, AlOmiri MK, et al. Predicting recurrent aphthous ulceration using genetic algorithms-optimized neural networks. Adv Appl Bioinforma Chem. 2010 May;3:7–13.

68. Maghsoudi R, Bagheri A, Maghsoudi MT. Diagnosis prediction of lichen planus, leukoplakia, and oral squamous cell carcinoma by using an intelligent system based on artificial neural networks. Journal of Dentomaxillofacial Radiology, Pathology and Surgery. 2013 Aug 10;2(2):1-8.

69. Lux A, Müller R, Tulk M, Olivieri C, Zarrabeita R, Salonikios T, Wirnitzer B. HHT diagnosis by Mid-infrared spectroscopy and artificial neural network analysis. Orphanet journal of rare diseases. 2013 Dec 1;8(1):94.

70. Ali SA, Saudi HI. An expert system for the diagnosis and management of oral ulcers. Tanta Dental Journal. 2014 Apr 1;11(1):42-6.

71. Sharma N, Om H. Usage of probabilistic and general regression neural network for early detection and prevention of oral cancer. The Scientific World Journal. 2015;2015.

72. Saintigny P, Zhang L, Fan YH, El-Naggar AK, Papadimitrakopoulou VA, Feng L, Lee JJ, Kim ES, Hong WK, Mao L. Gene expression profiling predicts the development of oral cancer. Cancer Prevention Research. 2011 Feb 1;4(2):218-29.

73. Shams WK, Htike ZZ. Oral cancer prediction using gene expression profiling and machine learning. Int. J. Appl. Eng. Res. 2017;12:4893-8.

74. Song B, Sunny S, Uthoff RD, Patrick S, Suresh A, Kolur T, Keerthi G, Anbarani A, Wilder-Smith P, Kuriakose MA, Birur P. Automatic classification of dual-modality, smartphone-based oral dysplasia and malignancy images using deep learning. Biomedical optics express. 2018 Nov 1;9(11):5318-29.

75. Shamim MZ, Syed S, Shiblee M, Usman M, Ali S. Automated detection of oral pre-cancerous tongue lesions using deep learning for early diagnosis of oral cavity cancer. arXiv preprint arXiv:1909.08987. 2019 Sep 18.

76. Ariji, Y., Fukuda, M., Kise, Y., Nozawa, M., Yanashita, Y., Fujita, H., Katsumata, A. and Ariji, E., 2019. Contrast-enhanced computed tomography image assessment of cervical lymph node metastasis in patients with oral cancer by using a deep learning system of artificial intelligence. Oral surgery, oral medicine, oral pathology, and oral radiology, 127(5), pp.458-463.

77. Hiraiwa T, Ariji Y, Fukuda M, Kise Y, Nakata K, Katsumata A, Fujita H, Ariji E. A deep-learning artificial intelligence system for assessment of root morphology of the mandibular first molar on panoramic radiography. Dentomaxillofacial Radiology. 2019 Mar;48(3):20180218.

78. Orhan K, Bayrakdar IS, Ezhov M, Kravtsov A, Ozyurek T. Evaluation of artificial intelligence for detecting periapical pathosis on cone-beam computed tomography scans. International Endodontic Journal. 2020 Jan 10.

79. Miladinović M, Mihailović B, Janković A, Tošić G, Mladenović D, Živković D, Duka M, Vujičić B. Reasons for extraction obtained by artificial intelligence. Acta Facultatis Medicae Naissensis. 2010 Sep 1;27(3):143-58.

80. Chen F, Liu J, Liao H. Image-guided and robot-assisted precision surgery. InArtificial Intelligence in Decision Support Systems for Diagnosis in Medical Imaging 2018 (pp. 361-387).

81. Zhang W, Li J, Li ZB, Li Z. Predicting postoperative facial swelling following impacted mandibular third molars extraction by using artificial neural networks evaluation. Scientific reports. 2018 Aug 16;8(1):1-9.

82. Bouletreau P, Makaremi M, Ibrahim B, Louvrier A, Sigaux N. Artificial intelligence: applications in orthognathic surgery. Journal of stomatology, oral and maxillofacial surgery. 2019 Sep 1;120(4):347-54.

83. Reddy CL, Mitra S, Meara JG, Atun R, Afshar S. Artificial Intelligence and its role in surgical care in low-income and middle-income countries. The Lancet Digital Health. 2019 Dec 1;1(8):e384-6.

84. Neuhaus M, Boeckmann L, Zibelius K, Zeller AN, Dittmann J, Spalthoff S, Gellrich NC, Zimmerer R. Utilizing artificial intelligence for surgical decision making in orbital fractures. International Journal of Oral and Maxillofacial Surgery. 2019 May 1;48:33-4.

85. Choi HI, Jung SK, Baek SH, Lim WH, Ahn SJ, Yang IH, Kim TW. Artificial Intelligent Model With Neural Network Machine Learning for the Diagnosis of Orthognathic Surgery. Journal of Craniofacial Surgery. 2019 Oct 1;30(7):1986-9.

86. Bur AM, Holcomb A, Goodwin S, Woodroof J, Karadaghy O, Shnayder Y, Kakarala K, Brant J, Shew M. Machine learning to predict occult nodal metastasis in early oral squamous cell carcinoma. Oral oncology. 2019 May 1;92:20-5.

87. Xie X, Wang L, Wang A. Artificial neural network modeling for deciding if extractions are necessary prior to orthodontic treatment. The Angle orthodontist. 2010 Mar;80(2):262-6.

88. Zhang YD, Jiang JX. Analysis and experimentation of the robotic system for archwire bending. InApplied Mechanics and Materials 2012 (121):3805-3809.

89. Takada K. Artificial intelligence expert systems with neural network machine learning may assist decision-making for extractions in orthodontic treatment planning. Journal of Evidence-Based Dental Practice. 2016 Sep 1;16(3):190-2.

90. Thanathornwong B. Bayesian-based decision support system for assessing the needs for orthodontic treatment. Healthcare informatics research. 2018 Jan 1;24(1):22-8.

91. Kunz F, Stellzig-Eisenhauer A, Zeman F, Boldt J. Artificial intelligence in orthodontics: Evaluation of a fully automated cephalometric analysis using a customized convolutional neural network. Journal of Orofacial Orthopedics. 2019 Dec 18;81(1):52-68.

92. Kök H, Acilar AM, İzgi MS. Usage and comparison of artificial intelligence algorithms for determination of growth and development by cervical vertebrae stages in orthodontics. Progress in orthodontics. 2019 Dec 1;20(1):41.

93. Patcas R, Timofte R, Volokitin A, Agustsson E, Eliades T, Eichenberger M, Bornstein MM. Facial attractiveness of cleft patients: a direct comparison between artificial-intelligence-based scoring and conventional rater groups. European journal of orthodontics. 2019 Aug 8;41(4):428-33.

94. Kajiwara T, Tanikawa C, Shimizu Y, Chu C, Yamashiro T, Nagahara H. Using Natural Language Processing to Develop an Automated Orthodontic Diagnostic System. 2019 May 31.

95. Dharmasena RA, Nawarathna LS, Nawarathna RD. Predicting cessation of orthodontic treatments using a classification-based approach. Biom Biostat Int J. 2020;9(2):61-7.

96. Shankarapillai R, Mathur LK, Nair MA, Rai N, Mathur A. Periodontitis risk assessment using two artificial neural networks-a pilot study. International Journal of Dental Clinics. 2010 Oct;2(4):36-40.

97. Nakano Y, Takeshita T, Kamio N, Shiota S, Shibata Y, Suzuki N, Yoneda M, Hirofuji T, Yamashita Y. Supervised machine learning-based classification of oral malodor based on the microbiota in saliva samples. Artificial intelligence in medicine. 2014 Feb 1;60(2):97-101.

98. Ozden FO, Ozgonenel O, Ozden B, Aydogdu A. Diagnosis of periodontal diseases using different classification algorithms: a preliminary study. Nigerian journal of clinical practice. 2015;18(3):416-21.

99. Thakur A, Guleria P, Bansal N. Symptom & risk factor-based diagnosis of Gum diseases using neural network. In2016 6th International ConferenceCloud System and Big Data Engineering (Confluence) 2016 Jan 14. 101-104.

100. Shehnaz AB. Convolutional Neural Network for Periodontal. Blood. 2017;25:50. 101. Jahantigh FF, Arbabi S. The use of artificial intelligence techniques for the Diagnosis of periodontal disease by clinical indices.2018

102. Lee JH, Kim DH, Jeong SN, Choi SH. Diagnosis and prediction of periodontally compromised teeth using a deep learning-based convolutional neural network algorithm. Journal of periodontal & implant science. 2018 Apr;48(2):114-23.

103. Krois J, Ekert T, Meinhold L, Golla T, Kharbot B, Wittemeier A, Dörfer C, Schwendicke F. Deep learning for the radiographic detection of periodontal bone loss. Scientific reports. 2019 Jun 11;9(1):1-6.

104. Kim JE, Nam NE, Shim JS, Jung YH, Cho BH, Hwang JJ. Transfer Learning via Deep Neural Networks for Implant Fixture System Classification Using Periapical Radiographs. Journal of Clinical Medicine. 2020 Apr;9(4):1117.

105. Rhienmora P, Haddawy P, Suebnukarn S, Dailey MN. Intelligent dental training simulator with objective skill assessment and feedback. Artificial intelligence in medicine. 2011 Jun 1;52(2):115-21.

106. Sadighpour L, Rezaei SM, Paknejad M, Jafary F, Aslani P. The application of an artificial neural network to support decision making in edentulous maxillary implant prostheses. Journal of Research and Practice in Dentistry. 2014 May 31;2014:i1-10.

107. Li H, Lai L, Chen L, Lu C, Cai Q. The prediction in computer color matching of dentistry based on GA. Computational and mathematical methods in medicine. 2015;2015.

108. Chen Q, Wu J, Li S, Lyu P, Wang Y, Li M. An ontology-driven, case-based clinical decision support model for removable partial denture design. Scientific reports. 2016 Jun 14;6:27855.

109. Mine Y, Suzuki S, Eguchi T, Murayama T. Applying deep artificial neural network approach to maxillofacial prostheses coloration. Journal of prosthodontic research. 2019 Sep 22.

110. Yamaguchi S, Lee C, Karter O, Ban S, Mine A, Imazato S. Predicting the debonding of CAD/CAM composite resin crowns with AI. Journal of dental research. 2019 Oct;98(11):1234-8.

111. Deniz ST, Ozkan P, OZKAN G. The accuracy of the prediction models for surface roughness and microhardness of denture teeth. Dental materials journal. 2019 Nov 28:2018-014.

112. Alvarez-Arenal A, deLlanos-Lanchares H, Martin-Fernandez E, Mauvezin M, Sanchez ML, de Cos Juez FJ. An artificial neural network model for the prediction of bruxism by means of occlusal variables. Neural Computing and Applications. 2020 Mar;32(5):1259-67.

113. Bhatia A, Singh R. Using Bayesian Network as Decision-making system tool for deciding Treatment plan for Dental caries. Journal of Academia and Industrial Research (JAIR). 2013 Jul;2(2):93.

114. Ali RB, Ejbali R, Zaied M. Detection and classification of dental caries in x-ray images using deep neural networks. In International Conference on Software Engineering Advances (ICSEA) 2016 Aug 21 (p. 236).

115. ALbahbah AA, El-Bakry HM, Abd-Elgahany S. A New Optimized Approach for Detection of Caries in Panoramic Images. International Journal of Computer Engineering and Information Technology. 2016 Sep 1;8(9):166.

116. Rhienmora P, Gajananan K, Haddawy P, Dailey MN, Suebnukarn S. Augmented reality haptics system for dental surgical skills training. InProceedings of the 17th ACM Symposium on Virtual Reality Software and Technology 2010 Nov 22 (pp. 97-98).

117. Su Yin M, Haddawy P, Suebnukarn S, Schultheis H, Rhienmora P. Use of haptic feedback to train correct application of force in endodontic surgery. InProceedings of the 22nd International Conference on Intelligent User Interfaces 2017 Mar 7 (pp. 451-455).

118. Fukuda M, Inamoto K, Shibata N, Ariji Y, Yanashita Y, Kutsuna S, Nakata K, Katsumata A, Fujita H, Ariji E. Evaluation of an artificial intelligence system for detecting vertical root fracture on panoramic radiography. Oral radiology. 2019 Sep 18:1-7.

119. Mallishery S, Chhatpar P, Banga KS, Shah T, Gupta P. The precision of case difficulty and referral decisions: an innovative automated approach. Clinical oral investigations. 2019 Aug 13:1-7.

120. Moghimi S, Talebi M, Parisay I. Design and implementation of a hybrid genetic algorithm and artificial neural network system for predicting the sizes of unerupted canines and premolars. The European Journal of Orthodontics. 2012 Aug 1;34(4):480-6.

121. Javed S, Zakirulla M, Baig RU, Asif SM, Meer AB. Development of artificial neural network model for prediction of post-streptococcus mutans in dental caries. Computer methods and programs in biomedicine. 2020 Apr 1;186:105198.

122. You W, Hao A, Li S, Wang Y, Xia B. Deep learning-based dental plaque detection on primary teeth: a comparison with clinical assessments. BMC Oral Health. 2020 Dec;20:1-7.

123. Tamaki Y, Nomura Y, Katsumura S, Okada A, Yamada H, Tsuge S, Kadoma Y, Hanada N. Construction of a dental caries prediction model by data mining. Journal of oral science. 2009;51(1):61-8.

124. Borra RC, Andrade PM, Corrêa L, Novelli MD. Development of an open case-based decision support system for diagnosis in oral pathology. European Journal of Dental Education. 2007 May;11(2):87-92.

125. Chang SW, Abdul-Kareem S, Merican AF, Zain RB. Oral cancer prognosis based on clinicopathologic and genomic markers using a hybrid of feature selection and machine learning methods. BMC bioinformatics. 2013 Dec 1;14(1):170.

126. Sharma N, Om H. Usage of probabilistic and general regression neural network for early detection and prevention of oral cancer. The Scientific World Journal. 2015 Jan 1;2015.

127. Chatterjee, S., Nawn, D., Mandal, M., Chatterjee, J., Mitra, S., Pal, M. and Paul, R.R., 2018, March. Augmentation of statistical features in cytopathology towards a computer-aided diagnosis of oral precancer. In 2018 Fourth International Conference on Biosignals, Images and Instrumentation (ICBSII);206-212.

128. Avuçlu E, Başçiftçi F. Novel approaches to determine age and gender from dental x-ray images by using multiplayer perceptron neural networks and image processing techniques. Chaos, Solitons & Fractals. 2019 Mar 1;120:127-38.

129. Alkaabi S, Yussof S, Al-Mulla S. Evaluation of Convolutional Neural Network based on Dental Images for Age Estimation. In2019 International Conference on Electrical and Computing Technologies and Applications (ICECTA) 2019 Nov 19; 1-5. IEEE.

130. Farhadian M, Salemi F, Saati S, Nafisi N. Dental age estimation using the pulp-to-tooth ratio in canines by neural networks. Imaging science in dentistry. 2019 Mar 1;49(1):19-26.

131. Hemalatha B, Rajkumar N. A versatile approach for dental age estimation using a fuzzy neural network with teaching learning-based optimization classification. Multimedia Tools and Applications. 2020 Feb;79(5):3645-65.

132. Patil V, Vineetha R, Vatsa S, Shetty DK, Raju A, Naik N, Malarout N. Artificial neural network for gender determination using mandibular morphometric parameters: A comparative retrospective study. Cogent Engineering. 2020 Jan 1;7(1):1723783.

133. 10 Best Artificial Intelligence Software (AI Software Reviews in 2020) [Internet]. [cited 2020 Sep 4]. Available from: https://www.softwaretestinghelp.com/artificial-intelligence-software/